Black Saturday

Black
Saturday

Alexander McKee

Illustrated with Photographs

Holt, Rinehart and Winston
New York

Only one decoration was ever awarded in connection with the sinking of H.M.S. *Royal Oak;* it went to Skipper Gatt of the drifter *Daisy II*, and no man more deserved it. Because there were no officers present in the mess decks, to testify to what happened there, a number of other men— some of whom are dead—did not, and could not, achieve any recognition for their actions. This book, based on the testimony of their shipmates, may perhaps go a little way towards remedying that. "Fearful lights that never beckon, save when kings and heroes die," wrote Aytoun of the northern lights which were said to have flickered earlier that night above Scapa Flow. Not all the men whose actions are recounted here were heroes; but some of them were.

My earliest memento of H.M.S. *Royal Ooak* is a Christmas card received from her when she was on neutrality patrol off the north coast of Spain during the Civil War; the sender was killed later at Dunkirk. My next connection with the ship was when I met her navigator about ten days after the sinking; he told his story extremely well, and I often wish I could have recorded it. Subsequently, I cut out and kept every reference to the event which I could find. Almost precisely nineteen years afterwards, I set out to reconstruct the drama of that night in Scapa Flow. My reason was that, although descriptions without number had been published, they were virtually all repetitions of the story told by Lieutenant Prien, the U-boat commander credited with sinking her; there was little from the British side. In the end, I found that I had some sixty witnesses, whose accounts contradicted the previously published stories at almost every point.

I have read, I believe, most of what has been written about the *Royal Oak* and have drawn upon it, here and there, where it seemed reliable; but those occasions were regrettably rare. It would however be astonishingly reckless to claim that absolute accuracy has been achieved throughout, in reconstructing a bewilderingly swift succession of events which ended in death for two-thirds of the participants. I have not been able to question every witness to every brief scene; if I had, the descriptions might be modified slightly. Memory is selective. In particular, identifications of one man by another, unless he knew him well, cannot in these circumstances be regarded as absolutely certain.

Except in the few cases where it is expressly stated that a description is second-hand, it is based on one or more direct eyewitness accounts, some of them written down very shortly after the sinking. To preserve the authentic atmosphere I have used an equivalent to the best radio documentary technique of modeling the descriptions very closely on the originals, even where they are not directly quoted. Much of the narrative, where it concerns direct action, is therefore not a history at all; it is the nearest possible approach to the real thing, an account of the sinking by the men who were there, with the writer's role reduced to little more than that of selection, arranging and cutting.

I have, however, taken advantage of the fact that I was soon in possession of a mass of material not available to individual survivors, to bring some pattern into what, for those concerned, was often fragmentary and confusing. For these judgments the sole responsibility is mine. That is also true of the analysis of the log of U.47, although each point was intensively discussed with the survivors and a few outside, but expert, witnesses.

ALEXANDER McKEE

Contents

Black Saturday

1

Death at the End of the World

The Romans called the northern islands Ultima Thulae—
the end of the world. As a matter of geography it was not
true, but as an expression of what it feels like to be there
as a southern stranger, it was, and is, exactly right.

When the Vikings landed on Orkney they felt sufficiently
at home to settle there; it was so like the wild and savage
coast from which they had sailed. Black, grained sheets of
rock rose hundreds of feet out of the bursting Atlantic; cut
into the cliffs by the pounding tides were great fiords,
known as geos, each one a white, whirling caldron of
screaming sea birds. Only a few withered trees, like hunch-
backed dwarfs, clung to the earth in the rare places free of
the pouring wind, and pricked skulls and bones of cattle
lay in the heather. Half the time, the hills had their streaked
backs in the clouds and gray vapor trailed over the black
pools still and reptilian, which pocked their summits; there
were valleys white with nesting gulls, which rose like a
cloud on human approach, their thousand voices sounding
like women lamenting "Oh, oh, oh!" When the sun cut
through, then the sea was revealed as an incredible waste

3

of water that stretched to an infinite horizon—desolation without end. As it was then, so it is now.

To the town-bred sentries of the second world war, condemned to guard this wilderness for how many years they knew not, against an enemy who would never come, the monotony eventually brought a lethargy akin to the "desert sickness" experienced by soldiers serving in the French Foreign Legion. The train bringing them back to the north, from leave, became the saddest train in the world; the southbound train, the happiest. The stretch of water, in the center of the circling islands, which they guarded, was eventually to become, as it had been in the first world war, the impregnable main anchorage of the British and Allied navies in European waters. But, in this sixth week of the second world war, its defenses consisted largely of what little had not been removed, or rotted away, during twenty years of peace and disarmament. In name only, was it still "Impregnable Scapa."

It was precisely because of the undefended state of the anchorage that, on the night of October 13-14, 1939, it was almost deserted; all the important units of the Home Fleet had gone, in the apparently endless process of being rotated from one insecure base to another, in the hope of evading attack. And it was because the main threat was considered to be from the air, that the 29,000-ton battleship *Royal Oak* was anchored in the distant northeast corner of the Flow, to which her antiaircraft (A.A.) guns could give protection, instead of being in the southwest corner, near the naval base of Lyness, which was guarded by the only eight heavy A.A. guns then at Scapa.

At midnight precisely the watches in the ship changed over, but Sergeant J. McLaverty of the Royal Marines continued to walk the forecastle for some minutes more, talking to Color Sergeant Harold C. Paice, the senior noncommissioned officer (N.C.O.) of the Marine detachment. Like most of the crew, both men were some seven hundred miles from home, which is nearly as far as you can get and still stay in the British Isles; both lived in Southsea, not far from the Marine Barracks at Eastney. Southsea now would be blacked out, but curiously enough they had never seen a blackout in a city; the thing was so new that it had replaced the weather as topic of conversation and material for comedians throughout the country. It was, indeed, the only sign of war.

Of course, Scapa was blacked out, but it made hardly any difference to the ring of barren, sparsely populated islands; the Flow was not like Portsmouth harbor, with a city on two sides of it. It was enormous, and almost deserted. The actual naval base, Lyness—which was largely a collection of huts and some oil tanks—was ten miles away and hidden behind hills; Kirkwall, the small town which was the capital of Orkney, lay four miles away beyond the bow. There would be a few drifters in that direction, tied up to Scapa Pier. Two miles away to port the old seaplane carrier *Pegasus* was anchored, the only other ship at all in that part of the Flow. There was no sign of her, because she, too, was blacked out. Blackout regulations for the Home Fleet, laid down by the Commander in Chief, Admiral Forbes, consisted of painting the riding lights blue, so that they were visible only from a distance of two or three hundred yards, and the fitting of "light-excluding ventilators" to the portholes instead of the glass scuttles. These ventilators allowed air into the cabins and mess decks, while preventing the escape of any light; they were not, however, waterproof. If they were to be submerged, the sea would pour through in a torrent.

Paice and McLaverty could dimly make out the nearest part of the mainland, which was half a mile away on the starboard beam, because the dark mass of the cliffs made a vague silhouette against the starlit night sky; but there was no moon, and the battleship herself was invisible from the Flow at anything over 250 yards. On nights like this her picket boat, returning late with the mail, had to steer a compass course towards her until the cox could see the radio masts on the hill behind her; knowing from there roughly where she lay, he would then alter course until, with luck, about two hundred yards distant from the battleship, her riding lights became visible. The night was calm and cold; the tide, running fast along the sides of the *Royal Oak*, was now going out, for it was more than two hours after high tide; the temperature of that black water on this winter night was 48° F., cold enough to shock and numb a man within minutes.

The *Royal Oak* had virtually no lifesaving equipment left; most of the Carley rafts had been smashed in a gale and the broken pieces were piled up on the forecastle, where Paice and McLaverty were walking; in an emergency, however, these would be better than nothing, and that was why they were there. McLaverty himself was the proud possessor of one of the few life jackets in the ship. He was proud of it because it was German, given to him by a prisoner from a Dornier flying boat which had been shot down while shadowing the fleet. It gave him a pleasant feeling of actually being in the war. But there had been no general issue of lifejackets yet and the crew of the battleship were without any personal means of flotation in the water. That did not worry them at the moment, because they were safely in harbor behind defenses which, so far as they knew, had proved impenetrable for the whole five years of the first world war. Anyway, to those who live in her, a battleship—even an old one—always seems far too large, solid and comfortable to sink.

The *Royal Oak was* rather old. Indeed, that was why she had been left in Scapa; she was now too slow to keep up with the rest of the fleet. Her value was reduced to that of a floating A.A. battery in harbor or as "long stop" in a complicated maneuver for heading off German warships, which was the role from which she had just returned; and no doubt she would have been useful for convoy work or coastal bombardment. She was one of the five ships of the *Royal Sovereign* class laid down under the 1913-14 estimates as cheap, coal-burning copies of the *Queen Elizabeths*. The *Royal Oak* was built at Devonport between January, 1914, and May, 1916, at a cost of just under two and a half million pounds. In appearance, like her sister ships, she closely resembled the earlier *Queen Elizabeth* class which, however, had two funnels (later trunked into one). The general layout was exactly the same.

Amidships, the hull was built around four Parsons turbines and eighteen Yarrow oil-fired boilers, the change from coal to oil having been made while she was still under construction. This vital part of the ship was shielded by what amounted to a gigantic, upturned tray of armor plate which was, in places, thirteen inches thick; it served to protect her propelling machinery from projectiles striking her deck and sides. It did not, and could not, extend very far below the waterline. The doors and hatches in this armored belt were, naturally, kept to a minimum and were themselves so heavy that they could be opened only by machinery.

At either end of the propelling machinery amidships was dispersed the main punch of the battleship, the reason for her existence: eight fifteen-inch guns in four turrets, two just forward of the engines, two just aft of the boilers. The guns were protected by armor which in places was thirteen inches thick. The turrets revolved on barbettes, again

thickly armored, which went down several decks to the
armored belt, so that the shells and cordite charges coming
up through them from the shell rooms and magazines below the waterline would be shielded during the dangerous
passage to the guns.

The shell room for each turret held 208 fifteen-inch shells,
the magazine next to it contained the appropriate number
of cordite propellent charges; from above, these were protected by the armored deck, capped by the barbettes and
turrets. If a single enemy shell or bomb broke through a
weak point to explode the cordite in a magazine, the shell
room would explode within seconds, probably setting off
the next room as well. The result would be a double bang,
a cloud of smoke half a mile high, and about three survivors.
It could happen accidentally, if the temperature of the
cordite was allowed to rise; a ship could blow up at anchor,
with no enemy near. To avoid a cordite explosion a system
of safety vents was fitted which would allow the burning
cordite to escape through the ship to the air, before it built
up enough pressure to explode. The result would be a trail
of havoc, of cindered corpses and terribly burned men
screaming in agony, but the ship would still be afloat and
fighting.

Below the waterline the *Royal Oak* had no heavy armor
protection for these vulnerable parts; there is a practical
limit to the amount of armor that can be put in a ship, and
a totally protected battleship would not float. Underwater
protection was by the lighter means of antitorpedo bulges,
or "blisters," added as an afterthought to the original design.
The result looked as if someone had sliced a gigantic sau-
sage down the center and stuck one half to the battleship's
starboard side and the other half to her port side. A torpedo
was supposed to spend its force on rending open the blister,

leaving the hull intact or, at any rate, not very much damaged.

The actual bottom of the ship was the most vulnerable part; and the Germans had in fact a not very reliable magnetic fuse for a torpedo which would explode the warhead directly under the hull; for technical reasons, this was not likely to be used in the shallow waters of an anchorage but, when employed in the open sea, immensely increased the effect of a torpedo.

The hull was, of course, divided into a great many watertight compartments but, as the ship was in harbor, not all the watertight doors were closed. On most decks the alternate doors, on opposite sides of the ship, were open, so that it was not possible to walk inside the *Royal Oak* in a straight line from bow to stern; it was necessary continually to cross over from port to starboard and then back again. This gave a measure of protection against the flash from any sudden explosion and at the same time allowed work to go on normally. But if the ship were to be holed unexpectedly and without warning, the flooding could only be localized by closing the remaining watertight doors—and that could only be done if there was power to operate the machinery or time enough for men to do the work manually.

In addition, the aims of the Gunnery branch, concerned exclusively with the problems of hitting other people, clashed frequently with the demands of Damage Control, responsible for the safety of their own ship, when hit. The latter might maintain that a particular opening should be closed, for protective purposes, while the former would insist that it be kept open, for ammunition supply. Gunnery was in the ascendant then, and Gunnery almost always won.

At about thirty minutes after midnight, Color Sergeant

Paice turned to McLaverty, and said he was going to turn it. McLaverty, however, walked up and down for a few more minutes. He did not normally stay up so late, but to-night he was First Duty and there had been one or two cases of overstayed leave, as well as men who had missed the boat for their own ships ten miles away at Lyness and had decided to put up for the night in the *Royal Oak*. One of them was a chief steward from the *Iron Duke*. Also, two men had been put into cells a few hours previously; they were directly below McLaverty, as he walked the forecastle.

Most of the crew, dead tired, had turned in early, glad to be back in the security of Scapa, where they could relax; to them the *Royal Oak* was something permanent, unshakable, unsinkable. McLaverty, who had joined the Navy in 1912, knew this was illusion. He had served before at Scapa, in the battleship *King George V*, and could remember still a night in July, 1917, when the dull roar of a giant double explosion rocked the anchorage and the whole Grand Fleet went to action stations, switching on their searchlights as if on a command. They swept across the water and settled on a spot where the battleship *Vanguard* had been; now, there was nothing, not even a ripple, merely a great cloud of smoke. McLaverty had been in one of the boats which had pulled away from the *King George V* to look for survivors, but they found on the water only a slimy coat of blood and oil. Other boats picked up a few men, he thought there had been three in all—and the ship's cat. A complete gun turret had been found on the island of Flotta, blown an incredible distance right out of the ship; and there were some pitiful bits and pieces, including a Marine's seabag.

What really happened that night could never be known, but the verdict had been, "lost by internal explosion." It had been impossible to say whether the cause had been an accident in a magazine, leading to the explosion of a shell room, or if the disaster had a more sinister implication. An accident in a magazine always is a possibility, but there had been already a number of British warships—far too many—destroyed in harbor by unexplained internal explosions, the *Bulwark* at Sheerness and the *Natal* at Invergordon were probably the best known. There had been whispers of "sabotage," hard to prove or disprove. There had been similar talk about the loss of the cruiser *Hampshire* which, with Lord Kitchener aboard, had blown up on what was thought to be a mine off Marwick Head, in June, 1916, shortly after leaving Scapa for Russia.

When McLaverty went below to turn in, in the early hours of Saturday, October 14, 1939, he was within half an hour of another Scapa Flow mystery; but this time he was to be an actual participant instead of a horrified spectator.

2

War Stations

The *Royal Oak* was a smart ship—possibly the smartest in the Navy. She was commissioned in style on June 7, 1939, her crew marching out of the Royal Naval barracks, Portsmouth, behind a band, wheeling to the right, down Queen Street, onto the Hard, and in through the Dockyard main gates to where the battleship lay alongside the Southern Railway Jetty. Her new Commanding Officer was Captain W. G. Benn, who had for his Senior Executive Officer Commander R. F. Nichols. Lieutenant Commander M. F. B. Ward was First Lieutenant and Torpedo Officer, Lieutenant Commander S. D. Roper was Gunnery Officer, Lieutenant Commander R. A. V. Gregory was the Navigator. Lieutenant Commander F. N. Cook was from the Royal Australian Navy. One of the lieutenants, "Pony" Moore, was an experienced submariner, doing his big-ship time.

Most of the crew were local men from Portsmouth ("Pompey" to the Royal Navy), though some came from Devonport, where the ship had been built, and a few were from the northeast coast. Not all were strangers to each

12

other; a number of them had just paid off the *Courageous,*
and so were shipmates already. It takes a little time for over
1,200 men to get to know each other, and shake down together into a team in a new ship; they were somewhat short
of that point when the end came.

But on June 7th no one had any idea that they had a
rendezvous to keep among the bleak northern isles. The
Royal Oak was destined for two and a half years in the
Mediterranean. She sailed first on a shakedown cruise to
Torquay and Portland, but events overtook her there. Hitler had already marched into Czechoslovakia, which was a
strategic move on his part, to outflank Poland; for the first
time he incorporated in the Reich a country which was not
German. He began, as expected, to press for the return of
the German part of Poland.

The Home Fleet sailed into Weymouth for a review—
which can also be a polite method of mobilization—but the
ships afterwards dispersed to their home ports to give summer leave. Two weeks later the *Royal Oak* sailed for the
last time from "Pompey," to take part in a Home Fleet convoy exercise. By the end of August the ships were concen-
trating at Scapa under war orders, though war had not yet
broken out. The communications ship *Greenwich* was first
in, followed by the *Royal Oak.* They watched the *Iron Duke*
—popularly known as the "Iron Duck"—come in. She was
Jellicoe's old flagship at Jutand, now partly demilitarized,
and serving as a training and depot ship. The Duke of
Wellington was nicknamed after the first ship to bear this
name, which was, literally, the first H.M.S. *Duke* to be built
of iron. When a hospital ship, the *Isle of Jersey,* also sailed
into the anchorage, glittering with white paint and red
crosses, there was a roar of joking: "Now we know there's
going to be war—the Admiralty are taking care of every-

thing." In spite of all the indications most of them found it hard to believe that another world war was upon them. There had been a similar "flap" the previous year.

Actual signs of warlike preparations at Scapa, other than the gathering fleet, were few and far between. There were three main, easily navigable entrances to the eight-miles-square stretch of water which is Scapa Flow—the Sounds of Hoxa, Hoy and Switha. Each was guarded by a single line of nets which looked rather like a row of lobster pots —these were the "flotations" which supported the two inch wire net. In the center of each line of nets was a "gate," which was merely a length of floating net which could be moved like a door, by two bar boats stationed on opposite sides of it, to let ships in or out. Daring submarine commanders who try to sneak through in the wake of a ship are usually dead submarine commanders in short order, because the trick is known. Small patrol vessels zigzag in the entrance as soon as the "gate" is opened, and as the ship passes through close up about her stern, watching for any signs of a submarine.

These defenses, however, were not as strong as they had been in the first world war, or as they would be again. It is perfectly possible for a submarine fitted with explosive wire cutters to go through a single line of nets; it takes at least two lines of nets to first slow, and then stop, her. A really impregnable floating defense consists of an "indicator" net (a sort of burglar alarm), or alternatively a controlled mine field, well forward of the main boom which should itself consist of four lines of nets. But most of this equipment had been removed after the first world war and had not yet been replaced; a bold and lucky submarine commander probably could have got through the booms at this stage of the war.

There were four other entrances to the Flow, all of them

on the eastern side, all close together, all narrow, and only one of them navigable. This latter was Kirk Sound, which is part of Holm Sound, where it divides round the island of Lamb Holm. The channels on both sides of this island had been obstructed by the sinking in them, during the first world war, of blockships filled with concrete. Those blockships were still there. They were not, however, covered by fire—there were no coastal batteries in position. There was a village—St. Mary's, or Holm—on the mainland side of Kirk Sound and a submarine coming past the blockships would have to pass this. This particular channel was, as it happens, not only navigable, but in use by ships of up to six hundred tons. The blockships had been sunk, not bow to stern, but parallel and overlapping, so that there was a zigzag gap—although from seaward, to the U-boat's-eye view, they would present the appearance of an absolutely continuous line of defense. That may have been deliberate, but in a new war in which air photography would undoubtedly reach out to Scapa, it was an omission which ought to have been repaired. In fact, plans were on foot to do this and a suitable additional blockship had already been earmarked by the Admiralty. However, it was soon to be sunk on its way north.

Local skippers considered it impossible to get through that channel except at certain conditions of the tide. It was not that there was not enough water, but that the water went through too fast. The Pentland Firth outside compresses the full power of the Atlantic between rocky walls, making it probably the worst stretch of water around the British Isles; this tide forces its way through Holm Sound with furious energy. To come in with the tide is—or rather, was, because the channel has now been blocked by a causeway—rather like riding a canoe down a Rocky Mountain river. The only practical method, in their view was to make the passage against the tide, thus slowing and steadying the vessel. This was particularly applicable to a submarine, which, because it has very little buoyancy, tends to make a piglike sort of wallow instead of a turn. It is easy enough for a submarine to go out of harbor sideways, if the current is right.

Very shortly after the *Royal Oak* arrived at Scapa, "Pony" Moore, who was divisional officer of the 120 boy seamen she carried, decided to make his own survey of the defenses. He had a look at Kirk Sound and came back to tell his friends that he, personally, would have no hesitation at all in bringing in a small submarine through that channel. And he forthwith made an official report to that effect. Nobody took very much notice, because it was thought he was inclined to exaggerate. More important, the Navigator, Lieutenant Commander Richard Gregory, also inspected the blockships in Kirk Sound and the wire cable stretching across the the gap at St. Mary's—and reported in the same terms as had Moore.

Anyway, the submarine was believed to be under control, because of Asdic, a piece of detection apparatus of which the Navy was very proud; a very much greater threat was believed to lie in the air, at any rate to warships lying at anchor in an underdefended base. According to information in the possession of the Admiralty, the Luftwaffe was capable of launching an eight-hundred-bomber attack on Scapa Flow—which meant one hundred bombers to every heavy A.A. gun there. This alarming news was sent to Admiral Forbes on September 7th. There was a tendency throughout the first few years of the war grossly to exaggerate the strength of the Luftwaffe, possibly a legacy from Mr. Churchill's "twenty thousand first-line German aircraft" which had caused much merriment in the aviation press just before the war. One editor who had been particularly

rude about this, was removed from his job in the first week
of the war.

The fact was that the Germans were strong, only by comparison with British weakness. Mr. Churchill at any rate
was not responsible for the latter, and his funny figures
were perhaps only a misguided attempt to spur rearmament.
At a pinch, by risking everything, and sacrificing bomb
load for fuel, the Germans could have put in an unescorted
attack by some four hundred bombers, But against this,
there were at Scapa eight heavy A.A. guns, no short-range
A.A. guns, and no high-performance fighters. There was a
Naval Air Station at Hatston, outside Kirkwall, but the
fighters there were naval machines and, like all naval aircraft, inevitably had a performance much inferior to that of
equivalent Royal Air Force (R.A.F.) types; they could not
keep up with the fast "evader" bombers of the Luftwaffe,
let alone catch them. The only part of the Scapa defenses
which had not been removed, weakened or neglected in the
peaceful years were the tides, which, fortunately, were beyond government control. The tremendous surge and scour
of the unhampered Atlantic—for nothing but three thousand miles of water lay to the westward—made mining an
almost impossible proposition.

To attempt to allocate detailed responsibility for this
state of affairs, without having access to all the documents,
would be presumptuous. The question is dealt with, to a
certain extent, by Captain Roskill, the British official historian, in *The War at Sea*. He exonerates the officers on the
spot, who had reported the deficiencies; passes the responsibility to the Admiralty, who had expressed themselves
satisfied and at the same time had delayed making up their
minds whether or not to use Scapa as the main fleet base;
and finally passes it on again to Mr. Chamberlain, for dealing a little too timidly with Hitler. There is no reason why

it should stop there; responsibility could be taken as far
back as Mr. Baldwin and spread to include the entire British electorate of the 1930s, less that small portion of it which
was actively in favor of rearmament. It could hardly be said
that the labor force was lacking—during that period there
were between one and three million unemployed rotting
out their lives in despair. The fact is that hardly anyone
wanted war with Germany, except one or two limelight-
seeking politicians and a handful of fanatics who camouflaged their possibly subconscious desires under hysterical
calls for peace and "collective security." The consequent
political confusion resulted in Britain's getting the worst
of all possible solutions—a world war, without the means
to wage it properly.

There were, of course, similar stresses and strains inside
Germany, with the difference that the man in charge was
an excitable, hypnotic Bavarian peasant, a master of mass
publicity but quite lacking in all the qualities needed to
walk the dangerous tightrope he had chosen to negotiate.

On the day he finally fell off it, the officers of the *Royal
Oak* were assembled on the quarter-deck to drink a toast,
"Damnation to the enemy." Shortly afterwards Winston
Churchill, who had now got back into the public eye as
First Lord of the Admiralty, came on board and made a
speech. Until then, there had been a certain air of unreality
about the war. One of his listeners, Stanley Saltmarsh, said
afterwards, "To me, as a young Marine, it was frightening;
but I felt if I stuck to my training, I'd get through. Probably for the first time, I thought of God and religion."

The *Royal Oak* now had an admiral and his staff aboard,
and her crew was being brought up to full wartime com-
plement. Rear Admiral H. E. C. Blagrove had recently been
appointed Admiral Superintendent of Chatham Dockyard,
but the outbreak of war meant for him a welcome opportu-

nity to command a Battle Squadron. Among his staff, who
also joined at this time, were Flag-Lieutenant G. Affleck-
Graves and "Bertie" Pyne, who was his chief writer. Most
of the Marines were very young, with not more than eighteen months service, so some thirty three-badge men were
drafted to the ship, among them McLaverty, whose service
went back to before the first world war. At the other end of
the age scale, Cadet P. H. Owen found his course of cadets
recalled from leave and some of them sent to Scapa; after a
few days in the *Iron Duke*, he joined the *Royal Oak*. Paymaster Commander J. R. Cundall joined in September—on
his birthday.

As the last shots of the Polish campaign died away, Hitler
turned his attention to the main enemy—the British fleet.
He could not match it at sea in a direct action because his
main interest, which lay in an eventual drive by great
armies to the eastward, had prevented him from building
anything like adequate numbers of ships. He was weak
even in submarines. But, as the former High Seas Fleet had
been scuttled—in Scapa Flow—what he did have were
mostly new, whereas what the Royal Navy had were mostly
old. Additionally, a German warship built for limited-
length operations in the North Sea and Atlantic Ocean
would always have a certain edge over a British warship,
designed to serve for years at a time in all climates, in
which crew comfort was necessarily a larger consideration.
A carefully integrated campaign in which surface warships,
submarines, mines and aircraft all played a part, might be
able to knock out within a few months a useful proportion
of the British Home Fleet. By then, he hoped to use his
armies to take for him forward bases in Holland, Belgium
and northern France, from which a war of attrition on
British sea communications could be waged at short range,
resulting if all went well in a peace by negotiation with

Britain and France. He would then be free to achieve his lifelong dream in the East.

He did not then anticipate that his limited-objectives campaign in the West would be delayed until the following year and that, when it finally took place, it would result in the total overthrow of all Allied forces on the continent.

On September 6th the first reconnaissance flight over Scapa was made, by a weather aircraft of Air Fleet II; and on the 7th the Admiralty warned Admiral Forbes, then with the Home Fleet at Scapa, that an attack by eight hundred bombers was possible. The photograph taken on the 6th, which showed both the main fleet anchorage and the destroyer anchorage, with the ships in them, reached the desk of Admiral Dönitz, commanding the U-boat arm, on September 11th. Dönitz wanted more information, and on the 13th sent out U.14 to patrol the Orkneys and report on the floating defenses, the coast defenses and the currents. When it got back, on the 29th, its captain said that he thought that a U-boat could penetrate Hoxa Sound when the "gate" was open. More reconnaissance aircraft flew over Scapa, so high that the sound of their engines could not be heard, out of range of the A.A. guns and beyond the reach of the naval fighters.

During the month, Lieutenant B. Keen R.M., was ordered to take about twenty-five Marines from the *Royal Oak* over to Kirkwall as a guard for some German prisoners. The prisoners turned out to be the entire crew of U.39, which, on September 14th, had put in an ineffective attack against the aircraft carrier *Ark Royal,* then at sea with part of the Home Fleet. After being counterattacked, the U-boat had blown her tanks and come to the surface, to the disgust of some of her crew. The U-boat captain expected to be allowed to go shopping in Kirkwall. After two days, Lieutenant Keen and his Marines took the prisoners on board the fleet minesweeper *Hebe* and, during the passage from Scapa to Scrabster, some of the Germans showed great familiarity with the Pentland Firth, pointing out various landmarks quite correctly. Obviously, Scapa was being kept under close observation from both sea and air. The prisoners were eventually handed over to the Army at Inverness.

By that time, the Germans had more than evened the score. U.29 sank the aircraft carrier *Courageous* west of Ireland on September 17th. However, it was not very long before the Home Fleet again provided Lieutenant Keen with some more work to do. Once again the bait had been the *Ark Royal* which, with two battleships, was escorting home from enemy waters a damaged British submarine. This gave the Germans the opportunity they wanted to try out their air force at close range on heavy units of the Home Fleet. At eleven o'clock on the morning of September 26th, naval reconnaissance aircraft saw that the force was being followed—three Dornier 18 flying boats were shadowing it from a distance. The *Ark Royal* turned into the wind and flew off nine Skuas, which were slower than the flying boats they were to attack. However, they put one down into the sea and the destroyer *Somali* picked up the crew. Very shortly after that, a single German aircraft dived out of the clouds onto the *Ark Royal* and planted a two-thousand-pound bomb thirty yards from the bow, which caused a cascade of water to fall on the flight deck. The pilot did not in fact claim to have sunk her, but the Propaganda Ministry did; they subsequently issued a booklet, supposed to have been written by the pilot, entitled *How I Sank the Ark Royal*. Their next in that line was to be a book, attributed to a U-boat commander, entitled *I Sank the Royal Oak*. In both cases, the date was right.

This time, Lieutenant Keen, who spoke no German,

found that one of the Germans from the flying boat spoke excellent English; he had been educated in England and possessed English connections. During the two or three days they had to wait at Kirkwall, this German invited Keen, quite seriously, to spend a ski holiday with him later that year. He judged that the French had no taste for the war and would soon throw in the towel, and a compromise peace would probably follow. The captain of U.39, it will be recalled, had also regarded the war as a nonserious matter, certainly not serious enough to prevent him from being allowed to go shopping in Kirkwall. McLaverty came out of it best of all, for one of the Germans, whose name he thought might be spelled Hinkenbein, gave him his Mae West. It was even more beautiful than the original, and self-inflating, with an oxygen bottle one side and a whisky flask the other.

The object of the stay at Kirkwall was to await the arrival of still more prisoners, this time from the blockade runner *Minden,* which had failed to to break through the Northern Patrol. Her crew, curiously enough, consisted of about thirty Germans and some three dozen Chinese. On delivering this lot to the *Hebe,* at about two in the morning, Keen found her First Lieutenant with his wits sufficiently about him to reply, "Sorry, no can do; not enough rice."

At about the same time, two pocket battleships had broken out into the Atlantic; to draw off pursuit, the Germans decided to create a diversion in the North Sea. They sent out the battle cruiser *Gneisnau* and the cruiser *Koln,* with nine destroyers. Anything small they could smash, anything heavy they could run away from; and when they ran away, it was to be towards the Skagerrak, where a U-boat and Luftwaffe reception would be prepared. On October 8th the force was sighted off Lister Light, on the Nor-

wegian coast, by an aircraft of Coastal Command. The
Home Fleet sailed from Scapa, split into groups to cover
the various courses which the German force might steer.
The battle cruisers *Hood* and *Repulse,* old but fairly fast,
formed the bulk of one group; the battleships *Nelson* and
Rodney, with the aircraft carrier *Furious,* formed the core
of another. The *Royal Oak* was much too slow to keep up
with either of these forces and was sent to patrol the Fair
Isle Channel with an escort of two destroyers.

The weather was extremely bad. The gale howled in from
the Atlantic and the *Royal Oak* went wallowing through it,
looking like an outsize submarine with only the conning
tower showing. Closed up at Number 2 gun of the starboard
six-inch battery was Stanley Saltmarsh, who had been in the
Marines four years and had never been seasick. He was
now. The only thing he could keep down were apples.
There was a terrible mess in the battery, the gun deck was
afloat most of the time, several of the guns were damaged
and jammed in traverse. Carley rafts were torn away or
wrecked; and the two escorting destroyers vanished in the
murk, losing contact completely. When the battleship
turned at the end of her patrol line and came back again,
the raging seas put the port battery completely out of
action, emphasizing the tight-lipped comment on this class
in Jane's *Fighting Ships,* the British authority on the subject: "They are fine ships, but suffer rather from reduced
freeboard."

For the men, it was misery, particularly as they had only
a hazy idea of what it was all in aid of; but the feelings of
the senior officers can barely be imagined. In good weather
the poor old battleship cruised at twelve knots; when
pushed, and rattling in every plate, she could just make
eighteen knots. And she was now alone, without any escort

whatever. A fine crew, almost all of them professionals, with many irreplaceable long-service men among them, were virtually wasting their time in a beat-up old battle wagon which should have been replaced by a modern ship years before.

On October 10th, Admiral Forbes—who had yet to sight the German ships—was told that they were returning to harbor. It was hardly surprising, in the circumstances, that Coastal Command had lost contact with them for some time and that the Home Fleet had been searching blind; the acid quality of the naval historian's comments on the R.A.F. seems hardly justified. On that day the operation was abandoned and most of the Home Fleet set course for Scapa.

They had barely arrived when a German reconnaissance aircraft flew over. The crew of the *Royal Oak* were so worn out with lost sleep and the struggle in the gale that they hardly noticed it, or at what time it appeared, but only that the battle cruiser *Repulse* was then anchored a short distance away from them, in the direction of Kirkwall. From German records it appears that this was the aircraft flown by Lieutenant Newe which took a number of excellent pictures at three P.M. on Thursday, October 12th. Imprinted on one negative must have been the outlines of the *Royal Oak* and the *Repulse*, anchored close together in the northeast corner of the Flow; and that picture was indelibly fixed on German minds thereafter.

But, after dark, the Home Fleet left the known insecurity of Scapa for its temporary bases in Scotland; with it, went the *Repulse*. The only major operational unit left behind was the *Royal Oak*—too slow to keep up, but still useful as a floating antiaircraft battery. The ship carried eight four-inch A.A. guns, as well as an array of short-range weapons; the guns' crews, under Lieutenant Commander Roper and

Petty Officer Stannard, had been well-trained in the last six months and would give a good account of themselves if the heavy air attack, which the Admiralty believed was being planned, should actually take place.

3

Unlucky for Some

On Friday the 13th of October, most of the officers and men of the *Royal Oak* were looking forward to a full night in—off watch, and in harbor; some hoped to get a few hours ashore. But a hard day lay ahead for most of them, repairing damage and storing ship.

That morning Lieutenant Keen went over to the *Iron Duke* for mail in the fishing drifter *Daisy II*. It was a trip he always enjoyed. The "Iron Duck" lay off Lyness, ten miles away, and there was plenty of time for a really heavy breakfast. The six-man crew of the drifter, all civilians, usually had four eggs, with lots of bacon—eggs were always plentiful in Orkney throughout the war. The master of the *Daisy* was Skipper John G. Gatt; a tall, burly man from Aberdeenshire, he was part-owner of the vessel, which was a big modern steam drifter of steel construction. She had been taken over by the Admiralty just after the outbreak of war and on September 17th had been detailed to service the *Royal Oak* whenever she was in Scapa. She acted as a sort of waterborne bus and truck equally capable of taking

26

liberty men ashore or bringing stores alongside. But, this morning, the job was mail.

The drifter passed the main fleet anchorage, some miles south of where the *Royal Oak* was lying, and ran in between the islands of Fara and Flotta, the bare, purple and brown hills of Hoy ahead. This part of Hoy, inside the Flow, was low lying and actually boasted a coastal road, but the interior was mountainous and trackless, some of the hills rising to over 1,500 feet. Some of them had curiously descriptive names, such as Whitefowl Hill and the Red Hill of Sneuk. Almost ahead lay Lyness, an untidy straggle of temporary buildings, topped by the cool white cross of the naval cemetery. Many of the dead from Jutland lay buried there, as well as Germans from the surrendered High Seas Fleet.

To starboard was a long stretch of water which served as the destroyer anchorage; a number of coasters, acting as fleet auxiliaries, were anchored there, as well as two destroyers. A little further north, opposite the island of Rysa, lay the battle cruiser *Derfflinger*, bottom up, the last of the German ships to be raised by Cox & Danks. To port was Switha Sound, with a boom draggled in the water between Flotta and Hoy; that particular part of Hoy was where the Norsemen first settled. In the Sagas, it is called Vagaland. There was here a great bay, like a fiord, which ran for five miles into the interior of Hoy. Its name was Longhope. Near its mouth were two sizable ships, the former Lamport & Holt liner *Voltaire*, acting as a depot ship, and the hospital ship *Aba*.

Off Lyness was the *Iron Duke*, partly demilitarized, with two of her turrets removed. The place of the after turret was taken by a hut—which was the post office. She acted as headquarters ship and, less romantically, detention center. All these ships were necessary, because there were hardly any houses, there was nothing one could even call a village. In summer, there were more seals than humans sunbathing on the beaches.

But even in July, anyone who dived straight in, without first getting used to the water, would come up with a scream, numbed with the shock. The Arctic Circle was not so very far away.

After her visit to the *Iron Duke*, the *Daisy* spent the rest of the morning helping to store the *Royal Oak*. As well as naval stores from Lyness, there was fresh food from Kirkwall and frozen food from a store ship. All this had been prepared in advance, ready for her return from sea. Sergeant G. H. Booth, who was in charge of the party of Marines helping to get the stores aboard, had received in that morning's post a cigarette lighter—a gift from his wife, Evelyn. Supply Petty Officer N. J. Finley, who was superintending the work, had less reason to be pleased—some of the rum was leaking. Leading Supply Assistant W. G. T. Batterbury, who was the junior rating of the big Central Stores amidships on the starboard side, had a hard day, as did his equal in rank, Frank Sims, whose job it was to check the cartons of eggs, butter, meat and so on, which were coming out of the supply ship. The *Royal Oak*, of course, had her own refrigerating plant; about the size of a small drawing room, it was forward, deep down in the ship. Close by, also in the bow, was the Inflammable Store. When work ended quite a number of the cases were left in the area outside the stores, so that men going to the forward "heads" had to walk round them. The same was true of the area near the after stores, in the vicinity of "X" turret.

Chief Engine-room Artificer C. J. Wilson who, by virtue of his job, got around the ship quite a lot, noted that

stores were being loaded at three points—through the
hatch in the forepeak by the torpedo area (the battleship
carried four twenty-one inch torpedo tubes in the bow),
by a gangway amidships to the Central Stores and by another hatch aft of the engine room, by the Marines mess
deck and the magazines. What he didn't like was that
many of the men coming aboard with stores were civilians;
in many cases there was no one even to show them the way,
which perhaps was why they simply left some of the stores
in the outside areas. They were all pretty well bound to be
Admiralty employees, like the crew of the *Daisy*, but then
again, the Irish Republican Army had recently been in
the news for putting bombs in mail boxes; it was silly to
give anyone half a chance. Perhaps it was this or, more
likely, some subconscious unease, but Wilson was suddenly
seized by an intense desire to get a flashlight; he determined
to buy one in Kirkwall when he went ashore later in the
day.

Friday the 13th was also pay day—and unusually large
sums passed across the pay table because, in addition to a
fortnight's pay, the men's half yearly settlement was due.
They felt rich; and some of them, by "lights out," expected
to be a good deal richer. But most men wanted to go
ashore and there were the usual grumbles because the
number free to go was small. Ordnance Artificer E. G.
Dommett, for instance, with the rest of the ordnance staff,
was hard at work in the port battery, housing six of the six-
inch guns of the secondary armament, which had been
damaged in the storm.

After pay parade, which was later than usual, the *Daisy*
took the liberty party ashore. It was a fine day, with a light
to moderate wind from the northeast, a great contrast to
the gales of the previous days, and there was a particularly
lovely sunset, even for Scapa. Among the lucky ones was

Stanley Rowlands who had, without his being aware of it, just been promoted to corporal; but he did not discover this until he reported at Eastney after survivor's leave. He went ashore with his chum, Jimmy James, who was keen to have a studio portrait taken; the picture was sent on in due course, but Jimmy was not there to see it. Stoker H. P. Cleverley could have gone, but swapped watches with Stoker Johnson, because Johnson was an Orcadian; consequently it was Johnson, not Cleverley, who was down below in the engine room from midnight onwards.

Wilson, when he got ashore, set out at once in search of a flashlight. He had longer at his disposal than the ratings, who would be taken back in the *Daisy* at eight P.M. But, because of the blackout, flashlights were in short supply; also it was late for a shopping expedition. In the end, he got hold of a damaged flashlight which he bought for a nominal sum; then, in great good humor, he put through a telephone call to his wife. She sounded worried. There had been news of air raids on ships in the North Sea. "Where are you, dear?" she asked.

"Can't tell you," joked Wilson, "but we're as safe as houses!"

Earlier in the afternoon some of the senior officers landed on the shore opposite where the *Royal Oak* was achored and went for a walk along the cliffs in the direction of the village of St. Mary's and the channel where the blockships were lying. Captain Benn and Paymaster Commander Cundall did not get very far, but Cundall thought that the blockships must have moved, the gap was so large. Engineer Commander J. W. Renshaw and Surgeon Commander G. L. Ritchie, M.C., went further, and began to remark on the wide gap between the nearest blockship and the shore. It seemed to Renshaw that there was ample room for a ship of destroyer size to get through. However,

they thought nothing more of it, assuming that the gap
was watched, either from the shore or by a patrolling
drifter.

When Wilson came back in the *Daisy* at nine P.M., he
went below to help the watch on duty in the engine room.
They were getting up steam, because the ship was due to
move at seven A.M. next day. The decision had been taken
at a staff conference held a few hours previously. Intelligence had indicated that an air attack on Scapa Flow was
impending and some of the lieutenant commanders had
pointed out that the ship's present berth was too vulnerable; they urged that the *Royal Oak* should either go to sea
or move to the main fleet anchorage, where a few antitorpedo nets were already in position. Other officers opposed this and Admiral Blagrove, who was still new to the
ship, had finally decided to move on the following day.

Rumors of the impending air attack somehow got round
and Leading Seaman H. J. Instance, who was earning an
extra 8d. a day as an Assistant Schoolmaster, found that
some of the 120 Boys (aged 14-17) carried by the *Royal
Oak* were taking this very seriously, coupling with it the
ill omen of the date. He tried to allay their fears. However,
those who had heard the nine o'clock news were in
great good humor. The British Broadcasting Corporation
(B.B.C.) were reporting Friday the 13th as unlucky for
the Germans—two U-boats had been sunk.*

The first watch had gone on duty an hour before—at

---

* This report was followed at ten o'clock by another claim: "With reference to the previous communique the Admiralty state that information had
just been received of destruction of a third U-boat today, Friday, October
13. In this case also the hunting craft were able to rescue a few survivors."
Churchill, in his memoirs, states that these reports were "not confirmed by
the post-war analysis"; that they came in while he was dining, for the first
time, with the Prime Minister; and that Mrs. Chamberlain most charm-
ingly suggested that he had arranged all this for their especial benefit.

eight P.M. As the ship was in harbor, liable only to air attack, the A.A. guns' crews were at general quarters. Lieutenant C. E. L. Sclater, as A.A. Control Officer, was on the
bridge. Cadet Owen was at his air defense position—halfway up the tripod. There were a dozen men aloft with bi-
noculars as air lookouts. The A.A. Pool, which consisted of
the spare hands of the watch who, in emergency, would
form ammunition supply parties, were sleeping in the port
battery; their duty petty officer was J. R. Kerr. As he was
also the divisional petty officer, he spent most of the evening in the office, making out lists of names for various
working parties which would go ashore the following day.
There were also a number of men watching over machinery in various parts of the ship—Leading Stoker T. H.
Jones, for instance, was in the dynamo room, below the
waterline near the after magazines. In all, some two hundred men out of about 1,200 were on watch, which meant
that most of the crew would be able to get a good night's
sleep.

After continual watch keeping at sea—four hours on,
four hours off—plus the gale, and then a heavy day repairing damage and storing ship, many of them were,
like Sick Berth Attendant R. G. Bendell, "pretty near flak-
ers." Bendell should have remained dressed, but he took a
chance and turned in soon after nine P.M.

The date had definitely proved unlucky for two mem-
bers of the crew. The *Royal Oak* was a gambling ship,
boasting a Fraz school, a Shoot school, and a Pontoon
school, as well as a Crown and Anchor school. Play normally took place in the Gaming Space, commonly known as
"Monte Carlo," actually the canteen. A rare breakdown of
security in the all important lookout system had occurred,
and the second in command of the Fraz school had been
caught by a member of the ship's police. Together with a

Marine, he was now in cells forward, with an armed Marine sentry outside the locked door. The Navy, in common with the other services, takes a poor view of gambling, observing justly that men who have so little money cannot afford to hazard it on games of chance.

It was ten P.M. before Skipper Gatt and his crew, who had brought back the last liberty party, could turn in. They secured the *Daisy* by bow and stern lines to the port side of the battleship, forward of the accommodation ladder leading to the quarter-deck and aft of the last gun in the battery. When it returned from the *Iron Duke,* the steam picket boat would tie up to the boom ahead of them; secured already to the boom on the other side of the ship was the big motor launch. All other boats were inboard, including the captain's gig, which was aft on the quarter-deck, ready to be painted next day.

Supply Petty Officer Finley was playing Monopoly in the small mess set aside for supply and cook petty officers. At ten thirty the last record was played over the ship's broadcasting system. As usual, it was "Goodnight, My Love." Finley finished his game and went up to the supply office, where he slept, fortunately for him. No one came alive out of that mess. The only other survivor of the group was Petty Officer Cook G. Calder, who was on watch.

Sergeant Booth was going round the ship, seeing to it that all deadlights were secured and all sea doors closed; he turned in at about eleven P.M., partly dressed, because he was Second Duty. Leading Seaman T. W. Blundell had just been promoted to acting petty officer; the other cox and crew were out tonight in the picket boat, collecting mail from the *Iron Duke,* so he was making the most of his new mess, to get in a quiet game of Pontoon. Petty Officer Kerr, having completed the rosters for the next day, left the divisional office and followed his usual routine of drop-

ping in at the police office for a chat with Regulating Petty
Officer Williams and Acting Regulating Petty Officer Beal-
ing. By that time, the mail had arrived, so he took it to the
mess, where he found only Petty Officer Scarff and Petty
Officer Oxley. That was the last he saw of the mess and
Petty Officer Oxley. At about eleven fifteen P.M. he returned to the office and turned in. The "Guest Night"
which had been going on in the gunroom broke up at about
that time, because the junior officers would have to be up
early next morning, in view of the fact that the ship would
be shifting to another berth at seven A.M.

In the officers' quarters aft Lieutenant Michael Benton,
R.M., had turned in early, but a small group were still in
the wardroom, playing Double Cameroon, a game in which
ten dice are used. In one straight throw, Lieutenant Keen
got nine Jacks and a Queen. "Now who's Friday the 13th
unlucky for!"

He took out a cigarette and lit it. Immediately, two
other officers asked him for a light, because they were short
of matches and the bar was now shut. Keen gave a light to
a schoolmaster and then to Surgeon Lieutenant Dickie, asking him if he minded being third. He didn't. An hour or so
later he was dead.

At midnight the watches changed over. Cadet Owen
came down from his air defense position halfway up the tripod and turned into his hammock in the officers' cabin area
just aft of the Marines' mess deck. Lieutenant Sclater went
to his cabin, which was right aft, under the Admiral's quarters. Leading Signalman W. J. Fossey came onto the bridge,
relieving an Isle of Wight man, Leading Signalman Burt.
It was a dark night, he noticed; he could just make out the
cliffs some six cables away on the starboard side as a faintly
darker mass than the sky; but, apart from that, there was
nothing at all visible.

Stoker T. H. Jones, who had been in the dynamo room, was relieved by Leading Stoker Watson; Jones went to the officer of the watch for permission to open the armored watertight door leading to the bathroom. After all the stokers who had just come off watch had had a bath, he closed the watertight door, and reported it closed to the officer of the watch. By this time it was getting on for one A.M., Saturday, the 14th. He got into his hammock, picked up two pages of an old daily newspaper which was lying around, and began idly to read through them.

The little party of officers in the wardroom had finished their game about fifteen minutes before. Lieutenant Keen collected the three letters which had just arrived for him and, after he had got into bed, settled down in peace to read them.

4

"Don't Worry—It's Saturday the 14th!"

At one o'clock on the morning of Saturday, October 14th, Leading Signalman Fossey had been on duty on the flag-deck for an hour. He began to shift the "challenges," the code letters used for challenging other ships. First he altered those on the starboard side, then those on the port side. When he had finished, he looked at the clock. It showed 1:04 A.M.

Precisely at that moment there was an explosion forward The flag-deck was part of the bridge, with a good view forward over "B" and "A" turrets to the bow, but Fossey saw no cascade of water up the side, which one would expect from a torpedo hit, especially in shallow water. He at once assumed that an aircraft had glided down over them, engines shut off, and that the explosion was from a bomb. On the heels of the explosion came a thunderous, rumbling roar, painful to the ears; the anchor cables were running out, out of control. That seemed to confirm the bomb impression; the cables were led inboard to a point on the forecastle well back from the bow and on the center line of the

36

deck. He reached for a signal pad and wrote down the time of the occurrence.

Most of those who were sleeping forward of the bridge were awakened. Chief Engine-room Artificer Wilson, whose hammock was well forward, under the torpedo area, heard an "almighty bang" which seemed to come from right underneath, followed by the roar of the cables running out overhead. He got up at once, took off his pajamas, put on his underwear, added the pajamas as an afterthought, then a pair of overalls, shoes and cap. Rough-and-ready dressed, he came out into the torpedo area, clutching his flashlight.

Able Seaman A. J. Farley, who had been sleeping in "A" space, on the lowest deck down under "A" turret, opened his eyes, rubbed them, and thought he was dreaming. A steel shelf near his hammock had been snapped in two. He pulled on his trousers and climbed to the deck above, where some ratings told him they thought it was an air raid. But no alarm had been sounded, so he climbed up another deck yet and stood outside the Sick Bay. The deckhead of the forecastle was gaping apart at the top and there were fumes about which had a very sickly smell. But all the lights were on. He thought the indications pointed to an internal explosion in the Inflammable Store.

Chief Stoker A. Lawrence was not merely awakened by the explosion, he was pitched out of his hammock by it. He sat on the deck for a moment, dazed and still sleepy, then was away up the ladder to the deck above, just under and slightly forward of "A" turret. He could hear a man screaming, somewhere forward of that, and saw that there was water escaping—a fine spray was being blown about, as if from a burst pipe. Then it dawned on him that the *Royal Oak* was in harbor. The explanation perhaps was some explosion in the Paint Store or a carbon dioxide gas

(CO_2) bottle in the refrigeration plant. That was where the screaming seemed to be coming from, and he made his way towards it.

Leading Seaman Instance slept in a mess about ten feet forward of the Boys' mess deck. The explosion woke most of them. Instance himself jumped straight out of bed, ran aft to the bulkhead and looked at the clock—it showed 1:04. He came back, calling out, "Don't worry—it's Saturday the 14th!" Then, as leading hand of the mess, he told them all to get out of their hammocks and get dressed, ready for action stations. The general impression was that they had been hit by a bomb from a high-flying airplane.

The explosion was felt more violently aft than it was forward; "the stern kicked about as though in a heavy seaway." Quite a number of officers flung on a coat over pajamas and dashed up on deck. Cadet Owen, rather bewildered, went to his air defense station under the armored deck, found it empty, and came back again. Lieutenant Benton, who had taken sandwiches with him to his cabin, in order to get to bed early, was still sleepy. He lay there drowsily, his mind going back to the German reconnaissance plane which had flown over them. "By Jove, that's a lucky one," he thought. But there was no drone of aircraft engines, only a number of orders broadcast on the ship's loudspeaker and a jangle of keys as someone ran forward.

Skipper Gatt, in the *Daisy*, was also awakened by the explosion. He jumped out of his bunk and went on deck immediately, to find the officer of the watch, a Marine, asking him what had happened. Gatt hazarded that it might have been one of the fifteen-inch guns firing; the officer said he thought it might have been something in the drifter. When Gatt denied it, a midshipman was sent forward to find out.

When Gatt was talking to the officer, he noticed something floating between the drifter and the *Royal Oak;* it was coming from the bow with the set of the tide. The officer of the watch gave an order for an Aldis lamp to be turned on it, so a midshipman went forward to the flag-deck and told Fossey to illuminate it. Fossey, believing that there were aircraft about, was reluctant. He replied, shortly, that he had a wife and child.

Captain Benn and Commander Nichols came on deck almost simultaneously, together with other senior officers. Someone asked if anyone had heard an airplane. Someone else noticed that the explosion had blown down a light-excluding ventilator from the wardroom and that light was showing. There was a shout for a man to replace it. Commander Nichols began to issue a stream of orders: for the *Daisy* to raise steam, for the picket boat to raise steam, for the launch to be called away. As Skipper Gatt's men tumbled out of their bunks to obey, the ship's broadcasting system began to call: "Away launch's crew"; "Magazine Parties take magazine temperatures."

The latter order sent the special temperature party, the gunners' mates of the turrets, and the gunners' yeomen down below, under the armored deck. The order was a precaution against a magazine explosion, but it sent them all to their deaths.

Captain Benn went forward with a fairly large team, to investigate. It included the second Supply Officer, Lieutenant Commander MacLean, who was responsible for the storerooms; Lieutenant Commander Roper, the Gunnery Officer; and the Chief Shipwright. Commander Nichols was delayed for a few minutes on the quarter-deck, giving essential orders and talking to Admiral Blagrove, who wanted to know what had happened. The officer of the watch, returning from forward, reported that the slip of the starboard cable had parted; the cable had run out to a

"clench." Then Commander Nichols went forward. Other
senior officers were making their way forward independently. One of these was Admiral Blagrove, who had been
joined by A. W. Scarff, his coxswain. Scarff, whose mess
was opposite the cable lockers, had just reported to the
Admiral that the explosion had been on the center line of
the ship, not at the side.

Lieutenant Commander Richard Gregory, the Navigator, came on to the flag-deck, wherer Fossey and the midshipman had now been joined by the searchlight crews.
He was a sharp little man, who missed nothing in his own
department and little outside; when he told Fossey to
switch on a twenty-inch searchlight, Fossey obeyed.
Played on the water on the port side, it showed up what
looked to Fossey to be the sort of straw in which whisky
bottles are wrapped. Looking down on it from the quarter-
deck, Lieutenant Keen noticed something white floating
among it—a sea-gull, or possibly a sailor's cap. Skipper Gatt
much lower down, saw now that it was a mass of straw
and pieces of wood. Then the searchlight was switched
off.

A number of officers went forward from their quarters
through the Marines' mess deck, where Stanley Saltmarsh
and his friend Barry Hawes had both gotten up. Others,
like Stanley Rowlands and William Owens, never got up
at all; they simply lay awake in their hammocks. As the
officers went through, one of them called out, "Sarnt-
Major, see everybody gets turned back in their hammocks."
Saltmarsh obediently got back and tucked himself up under the blankets; so did Hawes.

In the Marine sergeants' mess, one deck lower, the explosion had been felt more violently. G. E. T. Parham, a
gunnery instructor, found the ship shaking so much that
his head hit the deckhead. He got up and tried to wake

the other men, but was told, even by his pal, Bob Bottom-
ley, to shut up and go back to bed. "I don't believe in getting caught with my pants down," said Parham, "so I
dressed and went on deck." It was cold there, and there
was no sign of anything wrong, so he came down again and
lit a cigarette, waiting.

Sergeant Booth's awakening was equally violent—he
found himself suddenly on the deck, and got up angrily,
thinking that someone had been skylarking. But no one
had. Being Second Duty, he was already half dressed, so
he went up into the Commander's lobby where a number
of seamen were lining up to use the night "heads." They
were talking about an explosion forward, and Booth
thought at once of the two men locked in the cells. He tried
to get there by going through the seamen's mess deck, but
there was so much smoke that it was impossible. Because
there were so few hatches to the upper deck, he had to re-
trace his steps before finding a ladder. He went up that,
then walked right forward to the foremost hatch in the
bow. Below decks there was so much smoke, and such a
pungent smell to it, that Booth thought at first that a torpedo war head had exploded. There was no one in the
cell area—both prisoners had gone, and the sentry, too.
Thick, yellow smoke was coming up between the deck
plates. The torpedo war heads were down there, and also
the refrigerating machinery with its explosive CO_2 bottles;
he made his way aft, rapidly, through the seamen's mess
deck from which the smoke was now clearing.

Sergeant McLaverty had turned in about thirty minutes
before the explosion. As the duty watch came running forward, McLaverty put his head over the side of his hammock and said, "What's up?"

"Flood in the cable locker area."

That meant trouble right forward in the ship, where the

cells were, so McLaverty jumped out and went to find the Marine officer of the watch, Acting Lieutenant J. T. E. Vincent, who had been in the ship only about a week. "Look here, sir," said McLaverty, "if there's a flood in the cable locker, it may flood the cells as well. Shall I release the prisoners?"

Vincent said that he could, so McLaverty hurried forward through the port battery. There he met the Regulating Petty Officer, coming aft with the two prisoners and the Marine sentry. The screaming which Chief Stoker Lawrence had heard was actually one of these men hammering on the door and shouting to be let out. "You're released from arrest," said McLaverty. Then he turned to the sentry. "Take off your belt and bayonet and look after yourself now." Crime, or at any rate minor service crime, sometimes pays; one of the prisoners normally slept in the boat hoist area with Marine Sandford and a number of others who were killed. But the bad boy survived.

McLaverty hurried back to Lieutenant Vincent, reported the release of the prisoners, then went into the Marines' mess deck, which was directly below the after turrets. "Come on, lads, get dressed—out of your hammocks!"

"What—another flipping air raid!"

There were groans of protest. Then McLaverty picked, as an example, on fifteen-year-old John Priestley, a boy bugler. For three generations, his family had had at least one member serving in the Marines. The boy was still sleeping soundly, so McLaverty stood him on his feet, gave him a slap round the ears to wake him up, and told him to get on deck. He never saw him again.

Amidships, the explosion had not sounded very loud or important and the shaking of the ship, as the cables ran out, was not nearly so pronounced as at the stern. Also, the men were very tired. Petty Officer Kerr thought the noise was "like a large zinc bath dropping onto the deck of the wardroom bathroom." When Petty Officer Puddy told him he had heard that a CO_2 bottle had blown up, Kerr went into the port battery and saw the A.A. Pool turned out, in case a fire or cable party was needed. Just forward of the battery was a small mess for supply staff. Leading Supply Assistant F. G. Sims woke up, but not at all violently; if he had been in a destroyer instead of a battle-ship he would have assumed that they had been bumped by another ship—that was the sort of metallic sound it was. But the *Royal Oak* shook—and that made him think. She was 29,000 tons.

He simply lay awake, listening, as did the next man to him; the rest seemed to be asleep. Then the group of senior officers passed through, on their way forward, and he sang out to a seaman, "What's the panic?"

"Think it's an explosion in the Inflammable Store."

In the same mess, Leading Supply Assistant Batterbury was also awake; when a call came for the duty supply rating to go forward, that meant him. Taking with him the keys of the stores, he reported to Petty Officer "Wiggy" Bennett, who was standing by the trunk leading down to the Inflammable Store; with him were a number of officers.

In the starboard battery the explosion was similarly vague, so vague that some of the boys sleeping in the first three gun casemates did not recognize it as such. The running out of the cables or the piped orders which followed were what woke most of them. Seventeen-year-old A. W. Scovell wondered if he ought to get up—he was the Gun-nery Officer's messenger. "If they want you they'll pipe," said George White, from the next hammock. One or two boys got out, but when word reached them that the Ad-miral and Captain were already forward, investigating, they turned in again.

The deck below the starboard battery was divided into two messes—boys under the first three guns, stokers under the three after guns. That was duplicated under the port battery—with communications ratings forward and more stokers aft. A cross-passage connected the two stokers' mess decks. In the communications' mess, not a man got up. Leading Telegraphist R. S. Jones felt only a muffled bang and a slight vibration; one or two men stirred around in their hammocks, that was all.

When Chief Engine-room Artificer Wilson came into the stokers' mess deck, he found a similar reaction there. After getting rough-and-ready dressed he had gone out, clutching his flashlight into the torpedo area, where there was a strong smell of burning rapeseed oil. This was used for the emergency lamps and was kept in the Inflammable Store, below the waterline. There was no alteration in the trim of the ship so, if she had been holed, it must have been well forward. In the torpedo area he found Engineer Commander J. W. Renshaw with one of his warrant officers. "What do you think's wrong, Chiefy?" said Renshaw. Before they had time to discuss it, a seaman reported that the refrigerating machinery had blown up. Renshaw knew that was impossible. "Get the Salvus apparatus," he said to Wilson," then go down and see what's happened."

The apparatus, a kind of smoke helmet, was kept in the Central Stores amidships. On his way there, and back, he had to pass through the stokers' mess deck. Almost all of them were lolling in their hammocks, with their heads over the side, not taking very much interest. He suggested they get up, but no enthusiasm was shown. Danger or no danger, they would not stir, except on a direct order. Until then, they were content to "leave it to Chiefy."

In the starboard stokers' mess deck, Leading Stoker Jones did get up; having just come off watch, he was more

awake than the others, had indeed been awake, reading, at
the time of the explosion. He went aft through the bulkhead and climbed up into the starboard battery, where a
number of men were coming from forward. "It's full of
smoke forward," said one man, "you can't go that way."
Another added that a CO_2 bottle had exploded. Jones lined
up at the "heads," found the line too long, and turned in
again. All the others were back in their hammocks, except
for half a dozen stokers hanging about idly, waiting for
something to happen.

Even forward of the bridge, there was not much alarm;
the explosion had seemed violent only to those sleeping
low down in the ship, near the bow. Wilson had been
alarmed, and so had Able Seaman Farley. Farley had come
up from "A" Space, and was standing by the Sick Bay,
which was between "A" and "B" turrets, on the starboard
side. Commander Nichols came along, with the Master-at-
Arms, and others; Farley heard him say, "Get the men
turned in, it's only a CO_2 bottle gone up." The Master-at-
Arms came up to the little group of men clustered by the
Sick Bay. "Away you go, lads, it's nothing startling, turn
in."

Ordinance Artificer Dommett slept on the starboard side
forward, under the cable, but even he awoke "dreamily,"
gradually becoming conscious of people hurrying about
and of an "evil smell." He got up, promised two or three
drowsy people in the mess to tell them what had happened,
and went forward, where Commander Nichols and the
Chief Shipwright were already on the scene. The urinals
were shattered and there was chaos in the "heads" generally. The Chief Shipwright tested by holding his hand to
the mouths of the vent pipes which led to the spaces below
in the bow. It was impossible for him to hold his hand
there, because of the air pressure coming out. He reported

that the ship was holed and taking water. That looked like an internal explosion in the paint shop or a neighboring compartment, forward of the collision bulkhead and there-fore not at all serious in itself. Anyway, the lights were on; there would be no point in waking the ship for this or even of allowing spectators to crowd round. Dommett and the few others there were advised to return to their messes. Chief Stoker Lawrence, who had been awakened much more violently than Dommett, had already done so; after visiting the CO_2 and the "heads" he had decided that it was nothing serious and saw that the officers and damage control staff were taking action.

One of the first on the scene had been Lieutenant Com-mander E. G. S. Maclean, the officer directly responsible for the Inflammable Store. Instructing his stores Chief Petty Officer to collect the keys of the stores, he had made his way through the port battery, climbing over and ducking under the sleeping men. His account explains the apparent con-tradiction between flooding and smoke, for which there was plenty of other evidence. "The pungent and unmistak-able smell of calcium smoke and a thin smoke issuing from the Inflammable Store vent indicated to me, at any rate, that the store was already heavily flooded and that water had reached the torpedo calcium flares. These flares were used with practice torpedoes to indicate their position af-ter completion of a run. It also indicated that there was no general fire in the Inflammable Store, for if there had been the smoke would have been thick, black and oily."

Engineer Commander Renshaw was on the spot, having been called forward by Captain Benn. Renshaw had first inspected the steering compartment, below the officers' cabin area but had found nothing wrong. Then he had met Admiral Blagrove who had said, "Come and look at my pantry." The cup handles were still hanging from the hooks, but the cups themselves were smashed on the deck; clearly, the ship had had a terrific jolt somewhere. On joining Captain Benn in the bow he judged quickly that the Inflammable Store was flooding but that only one compartment was affected and that the flooding could therefore be controlled. He suggested to Captain Benn that the compartments next to the Inflammable Store should be inspected, to see if the bulkheads were holding and then gave orders for the watertight doors leading to the capstan area to be opened up.

Able Seaman Farley was uneasy; he felt there was more to come. He hung about, many decks down, in "A" space, then made his decision. When he got back to the Sick Bay, he stood by the door, talking to the solitary patient there. Bendell, the sick berth attendant on duty, had never heard the explosion at all; he had been awakened by a man who wanted a small cut on his leg dressed. "How did you do that?" asked Bendell. The man explained that he had been blown out of his hammock. Bendell dressed his cut, took a look outside where there was nothing unusual, except for an odd, cloying smell, and then got back into his cot. "See the M.O. in the morning," said Bendell. "Don't be a bloody fool," replied the man, "the ship's sinking." Bendell thought he was "wet," turned over, and went to sleep.

Supply Petty Officer Finley, who slept in the victualing office, high up behind "B" turret, had felt the explosion sufficiently to go down to the main deck, where he heard the "buzz" about the CO_2 bottle. If true, that was his pigeon— the refrigerator held fourteen days' supply of fresh food. But he found only little wisps of blue smoke from the direction of the cable locker area and had to put up with jokes about the job he would have in the morning, putting the bits of beef together again.

Batterbury now saw a man go down the trunk—rather

like an elevator shaft—which led from the upper deck, just forward of the antiflash screens, to the capstan area and below-waterline compartments. It was in fact a chief stoker sent down by Renshaw. Batterbury thought he was a very brave man, and had the impression he had volunteered. According to Batterbury's recollection, it was at this point that he thought he saw a flash or flame coming up the trunk, certain to engulf the man before he could possibly climb up again. Possibly he may have been confusing the sequence, for the chief stoker was doomed, and may well have been the first man to die in the *Royal Oak*. Anyway, Batterbury was sufficiently shaken by whatever it was he saw, to run aft to warn his friends. He burst into the Supply mess, shouting to Leading Supply Assistant Hyde, "Come on, Jekyl, get up, there's trouble forward!"

"Jekyl" made no move to get up. He only grunted sleepily. "If the ship's going down, put me in the rum tub, I'll drown in rum."

5

"The Bloody Ship's Going to Turn Over"
(Forward)

At least twelve minutes, but not more than thirteen, had elapsed since the explosion. In that time, the senior officers had dressed, gone forward, and decided that, as the breathing pipe from the Inflammable Store was freely venting air, that particular compartment was flooding. The Inflammable Store was a place where a small internal explosion was possible and, indeed, Paymaster Lieutenant Commander E. G. S. Maclean, responsible for the store, afterwards told Lieutenant Keen that he was at that time thinking up answers for his court martial.

No one could know then that the stem and keel of the ship had been blown away in the Paint Store area—only divers could ascertain that. Even if it had been known, it would not have indicated mortal injury to the *Royal Oak*. The bow, where the hull is narrow and the compartments small, can take a good deal of damage without even affecting the trim of the ship, as it had in this case. On the evidence available, there was no reason for alarm.

Most of the crew were still in their hammocks, a good many of them asleep; among those who had got up there was a general desire to visit the night "heads," which were on the port side, below the wardroom. Nearby was a hatch leading down to the mess deck and workshops. Dommett joined the line; well ahead of him were Instance, Able Seaman Hancock, and Ordinary Seaman Hearn. Instance had donned trousers and service jersey; had he not done so, he would not have survived the next thirty seconds.

On the opposite side of the ship Paymaster Commander J. R. Cundall, who had put on trousers, monkey jacket and scarf over his pajamas, was walking forward through the starboard battery; he was slightly better protected than Instance, because he had put on his cap. Petty Officer Kerr, who had found the line at the "heads" too formidable for him, was standing outside the office, talking to Petty Officer Puddy. Finley was nearby, idly wondering if there was anything for him in the mail office.

Alongside, in the drifter, Skipper Gatt was still on deck, standing with the cook by the hatch forward. The score or so of officers, who had thrown greatcoats over their pajamas and come on the quarter-deck, was now reduced to about eight. Among this group, by now rather cold, were Flag-Lieutenant Affleck-Graves, Lieutenant Keen, and Midshipman R. P. Pirie. Lieutenant C. E. L. Sclater had arrived on deck some time after everyone else, but, on being told it was only an explosion in the Paint Store, had gone below again. Cadet Owen had been advised to turn in again and Lieutenant Benton, still sleepy, had never got out of his bunk at all.

Directly under the quarter-deck, McLaverty and Booth were trying to wake the Marines. There were sleepy protests of, "Don't be so bloody wet!" and half of them turned over, and tried to get off to sleep again. Booth sang out, "Stop arguing the point—everyone out of his hammock!"

At that moment, Lieutenant Keen was standing by the accommodation ladder and looking forward and to starboard. He heard a vague thump and saw a great column of white spray go up as high as, if not higher than, the spotting top, apparently almost in line with "B" turret. The ship shuddered violently and Dommett, outside the "heads" saw lamp fittings and bulkheads shaking and moving as if made of cardboard and yet still remain in position. Fossey, on the flag-deck, looked at the clock, reached for the signal pad, and wrote—"1:16."

Below him, on the port side abaft "B" barbette, Richard Gregory, the Navigator, and Bruce Ward, the First Lieutenant, were just about to go down the hatchway there, Gregory saw a vivid glow on the starboard side and a huge gout of water thrown high in the air. It fell back on deck and rushed across, four inches deep. "Hell, I've got my patent leather shoes on!" was his first reaction. Ward sang out to everyone to lie down, but Gregory stood there, not liking the idea of the cold water, and out of habit, looked at his watch. It showed 1:17, thirteen minutes after the first explosion. Glancing vaguely at the sky, for he still thought it was air attack, he saw the mast, and realized that the battleship was already listing perceptibly.

Batterbury turned round and ran back to the mess, to be with his pals; Bendell was blown or thrown out of his cot in the Sick Bay; Finley shouted, "That's no CO_2 room—that's a torpedo!" and ran for the nearest ladder, kicking his shoes off as he did so. Lawrence, several decks down, was pitched out of his hammock and, as he lay there dazed, heard water pouring in and the rumbling of gear as it was swept away by the torrent. The stokers jumped out of their hammocks, and Jones managed to get through the door in the bulkhead aft and halfway up the ladder. Instance, who was now inside the "heads" and just about to go out, remarked to Hearn, "We'll be going back to 'Pompey' for a refit, if this goes on."

At the moment of this explosion, Admiral Blagrove and his Coxswain Scarff, were abreast of "B" turret, on their way forward. Scarff, who survived, recalled that they both momentarily looked up at the sky, thinking the explosion might have been from a bomb. "The Admiral then remarked, 'We provisioned ship today; what may you be thinking?' I replied, '*Vanguard*.' He then ordered me to tell the Captain to abandon ship, to get the men out of the ship, and to see what the trouble was."

Down below in the bow, waiting for Wilson to bring the Salvus apparatus, Lieutenant Commander Maclean was standing next to "Pony" Moore, the submariner, who was responsible for the 120 boys carried in the *Royal Oak*. "This is getting bloody unhealthy," said Moore. "I'd better go and see what my boys are doing." That was the last Maclean saw of him.

About fifteen seconds later—it may even have been as much as forty-five seconds later—Lieutenant Keen, still standing by the accommodation ladder, heard two almost simultaneous thumps, which might have been two explosions almost together or one very large one. This time, there was no spray—merely a thick black cloud of smoke, with clearly defined edges, drifting slowly towards him. He thought it was probably atomized fuel oil from the tanks on the starboard side. On that, he and the other officers turned and "ran like riggers" to the back end of the quarter-deck, in case there should be any fragments flying about. Midshipman Pirie, in a narrative published shortly afterwards in the magazine of his old school, Ardvreck, wrote, "This explosion was much more violent than its predecessors, and a great pall of black smoke hung over the ship. There was also a frightful smell of burnt explosive, and the ship started heeling over quickly."

This explosion appeared to Pirie to be just forward of the mainmast—and did indeed turn the starboard engine room, No. 1 boiler room and the Central Stores into a chaos of wreckage, opening them to the sea. The boys' mess deck and both stokers' mess decks caught fire, killing most of the boys and a great many of the stokers.

The little group of officers, now right aft on the quarter-deck, got up and began to unship the Captain's gig, which was on its chocks there; it was difficult because the ship, with the utmost deliberation, was rolling slowly over to starboard, shaking and shuddering as the water rushed in and altered her trim from moment to moment. While they were doing this, a final violent explosion occurred, apparently right under the Marines' mess deck. Skipper Gatt saw the blast of it go right to the maintop, and then another cloud of black smoke rolled up and began to drift towards the little group of officers struggling with the gig. The battleship was now heeled over about 15° to starboard. Within a matter of minutes the sixty-odd light-excluding ventilators on that side would be submerged, with water pouring in through them. On that explosion, too, the lights had failed, so that all below decks was in darkness, except for the glow of the fires; the broadcasting system had been put out of action and the senior officers forward were cut off from all possibility of command. The only senior officer anywhere near the quarter-deck was Paymaster Commander Cundall, and he was lying, dreadfully burned, in the starboard battery.

The third explosion of this salvo had not only caused the lights to fail, but had set an after magazine on fire. The burning cordite did not explode, it simply swept through the vents, seeking the open air. On the starboard side, it caught Leading Stoker Jones as he was halfway up the ladder, then hit Cundall as he was struggling to get out, through the blackout curtains, onto the quarter-deck. On the port side, by the "heads," Dommett saw an orange pillar of glittering flame soar up the hatch. He cried, "Scramble—cordite!" and ran for the quarter-deck. Instance, just coming out of the "heads," ducked back inside but the flame followed him in and swept round and round inside while he crouched in agony, trying to shield his face and neck. In the Marines' mess deck, Sergeant Booth saw the flame coming at him—"It was like looking into the muzzle of a blow lamp, the flame was bright orange outside and an intense blue inside."

The flame roared about inside the ship aft, between the "heads" and the Marines' mess deck; part of it escaped to the open air through the blackout curtains leading from the port battery onto the quarter-deck, and vanished. Lieutenant Benton, who had leaped out of his bunk, saw, through a partly opened watertight door leading to the Marines' mess deck, the flame coming at him; but the door was somehow slammed in his face at the last moment. Leading Stoker Jones was knocked off the ladder leading to the lobbies near the quarter-deck by the first sweep of the flame, then was engulfed once more as the flame traveled back.

All this happened, according to many witnesses, within a space of less than a minute; others, including Fossey and Skipper Gatt, who were well clear of the explosions and of the flame, thought there were distinct gaps between explosions, of two minutes or more. The group of officers on the quarter-deck, however, thought the gaps were of about fifteen seconds or so. Inside the ship, men were even more confused, many of them were not even quite sure how many

(Courtesy of Wright & Logan)

The battleship Royal Oak.

At left, a plaque bearing battle honors of the ships which have borne the name *Royal Oak*. At right, a view of the *Royal Oak* showing the anchor cables which ran out after the first explosion and the fore hatch leading down to the Inflammable Store. Below, the *Pegasus*, bought by the Royal Navy in 1914 as a seaplane carrier and until the 1930's known as *Ark Royal*.

(Courtesy of Ferdinand Urbahns)

The submarine in the foreground is *U-Boat 47*, commanded by Prien; the ship in the background is the *Scharnhorst*. The picture was taken at Kiel in October, 1939.

The attacker relaxes—an informal picture of Prien (left) just returned from a tour of duty.

Prien's claims—only much later could they be put to the test—seized the imagination of the world. On his safe arrival back, he received the congratulations of Grand Admiral Raeder (above). And this was but a prelude to the honors to come. The Führer himself sent for the crew, congratulated each man personally, and decorated Prien with the Knights Cross of the Iron Cross (below).

Sick Berth Attendant R.G. Bendell, the ship's unofficial photog-
rapher.

Petty Officer J.R. Kerr, who
swam two miles to the *Pegasus*
in spite of severe burns.

Able Seaman A.J. Farley, who
was hurled into the air as the
Royal Oak turned completely
over.

Above, a scene of reunion following the disaster. Below, several wives with children anxiously await the arrival of *Royal Oak* survivors.

Most of these survivors, marching to Lyness naval cemetery for the funeral on October 16th, were picked up naked or near naked and are shown wearing the overalls and canvas shoes issued in the *Voltaire*. In the *Royal Oak* section of the R.N. War Memorial at Portsmouth, shown below, are recorded the names of all those killed and missing. Each year, on October 14th, fresh flowers are placed in an urn bearing the words "Lost on *Royal Oak*."

explosions there were. Few, very few, thought they were under attack; the explosions, violent but muffled, were coming from the direction of the storerooms and outside areas where stores had been put.

Wilson, carrying the Salvus apparatus, had almost reached the torpedo area when the explosions began. The first lifted the deck underneath him. Blurred, "as though in a film," he saw pipes and water beneath his feet. As the last explosion thundered aft, the lights went out, and Wilson felt a great wind which more or less blew him, still on his feet, aft towards the midships galley.

As he went, half blown half running, it was hard to keep upright. With all dark below, the ship had begun to heel slowly and remorselessly over to starboard. It was hard to find the doors, harder still to open them, because they were no longer vertical. Several times, Wilson found himself across the diagonal of a door before he had reached out to open it. The ship was really turning now, and he knew he had a long way to go. His goal was a ladder by the galley, leading to the upper deck. About forty men were struggling round it; milling, shouting, cursing, unable to see what they were doing.

Wilson was blown at them by the wind, out of the darkness, like a benevolent Buddha, flashlight in hand. It was the one he had gone to so much trouble to buy. As soon as he flicked it on, the men had no further trouble—"they went up that ladder like a sea of humanity." Wilson went up with them; carried up in the rush or blown up by the blast, he seemed not to tread on the ladder at all. Somewhere in this jam was Leading Supply Assistant Sims; when he reached the ladder there was an explosion, and the blast took him right up, as if he were walking on air.

Batterbury was also struggling to get up the ladder. The second explosion had sent him running from forward to his

chums in the mess, which was near the ladder. He only had
a hundred yards to go, but some of the watertight doors
were closed for damage control purposes and others were
slamming to with the heel of the ship; it was impossible to
go in a straight line.

A door slammed behind him, crushing the head of a
man who was trying to get through it. Batterbury saw
his eyes and tongue sticking out, then came the sound of
the third explosion, and the lights failed. He ran on. The
antiflash curtains in the battery aft were aflame and people
were pouring up from the stokers' mess deck below, "hol-
lering and howling about men being on fire down there."
This new crowd of men, many of them dazed with horror,
scrambled for the ladder. It was, said Batterbury dryly,
"survival of the fittest." The fear of being trapped inside
the heeling ship was overwhelming. Batterbury himself was
frantic to get a foot on the ladder.

At the very top of the ladder stood an old man, a yeo-
man of signals or chief telegraphist, he thought. Almost
certainly, it was Commissioned Telegraphist Hughes-
Rowlands, who was generally regarded as being rather
ineffective. He was calling out, "Take it easy . . . keep
steady," and striking matches to show men the way up.
They poured past him into the galley, and made straight
for a door leading on to the weather deck. Still the old man
stood there, striking his matches, and calling out, "Keep
steady, lads."

The ship was heeled over to 45° or more now; within a
minute or so it must turn completely over and take them
with it to the sea bed, alive and trapped. Batterbury was
still at the bottom of the ladder, shoving and pushing.
There was the roar of another explosion, the deck plate simply lifted up, and he went straight up the ladder without
touching the rungs at all.

The chief stokers' mess, which was on the starboard side under the Sick Bay, was flooded almost at once. Lawrence, blown out of his hammock by the second explosion, could see that the cover of the magazine hatch had been lifted and that water was coming through it. It burst and boiled among the men there and Lawrence, with three others, clung to the ladder to avoid being swept away. As the inrush lost its first momentum, Chief Stoker W. H. Aplin came floating towards them on a cushion; when he reached the ladder, he calmly stepped off, a lot drier than they were.

The water trapped at least four men in the cross-passage, Lawrence thought, and not all of those with him managed to get up the ladder. Aplin was one; he survived the *Royal Oak*, to lose his life off Norway a few months later.

At the top of the ladder was an area near the Sick Bay and yet another ladder, which led on to the deck by the forward turrets. Lawrence joined the line of men beginning to pile up at the bottom of that heeling ladder. The hatch cover above was down, so that those at the top were escaping singly and slowly through the manhole in the center of it, pushed up by the press from below like corks out of a bottle. None of them thought to stop for a moment and open the main hatch cover, so that a rush of men could get through it; instead, they were running for the side. Even the manhole exit was continually being blocked.

The reason for this was that, just below the hatch cover, was a slab of two-inch armor plate which came out on runners, when a toggle was pulled, just like an extension from a table, to complete the armor protection of the deck. As the heel to starboard increased, so the armor plate began to slide across the opening; to keep it back, someone had to hold down a toggle. That someone, if he stayed too long, was going to lose his life. No one stayed very long; they

held down the toggle for a few others to go up, then they
left it and joined the line.

Blundell's hammock was directly under this ladder, but
he was one of the last in the line. He had been dazed by
the second explosion, which had caught him as he was
reaching for his trousers. "It was really something. I was
in the *Ark Royal* when she was torpedoed in the Mediterranean, but that was nothing in comparison, not the same
sort of thing at all. This was as if some giant had got hold
of the ship and shook it—a 29,000-ton battleship!"

Bendell, who was at that moment flat on his back on the
deck of the Sick Bay, a few yards away, would have
agreed. "It was a hell of a bang—I dreamt about it for ages
afterwards." He simply lay there, for some minutes,
stunned.

Able Seaman Farley, who had been at the door of the
Sick Bay, was quick off the mark. Already uneasy, even
after that minor first explosion, he had marked down an escape route which avoided the ladder. The terrific impact
of the second explosion set him off like a runner from the
starting pistol. Quickly, he weaved in and out, avoiding
dead ends where watertight doors were shut. A third explosion sent after him a flash, which he saw, and a blast
wave, which he felt; it seemed to come from the boys'
mess deck, and put that part of the ship in darkness.

He scrambled up a ladder into the recreation space,
with not far to go. All mess utensils and gear now began to
fall off the tables and roll down the incline of the deck.
Down below, he heard a man dashing about in the darkness, bumping into bulkheads, apparently in a blind panic.
Farley was afraid, but he was keeping his head; he could
not walk to the guardrails at the ship's side, the angle of
heel was too steep for that, so he crawled, pulling himself
up the deck.

It could have taken him only two or three minutes, but, back at the ladder, men were still struggling and pushing to get up. A hatch in the deck of a warship, exposed to plunging fire, is a weak point, so the number is kept to a minimum. The bulk of her crew—1,200 men—had only about five minutes in which to funnel themselves through a very small number of openings onto the deck. It simply could not be done. The decision to treat the first explosion as what it appeared to be, however correct it may have seemed at the time, doomed nearly eight hundred men. They were still in the ship when she rolled over. Some of them never even found the ladders; blundering about in the dark, they lost themselves fatally inside the hull. Others were below the armored deck and, when the power failed, were unable to open the heavy armored hatches; completely trapped, they could only wait for the end in darkness. Other men were trapped and pinned, according to survivors and the testimony of divers, by various movable gear inside the ship sliding on to them.

Not less terrifying to the men inside her was the absolute silence. The humming of machinery and fans had ceased; the ship felt dead. And she was going over. "The steady remorseless rolling over of the ship was a horrible sensation," said Blundell, "because you couldn't do a blind thing about it. As we milled round that ladder, with varying degrees of impatience, I remembered the pipe for the magazine parties to go down, and I thought, 'Poor beggars!' "

There was a sudden shout of "Try the ports!"

Most likely, Chief Stoker Lawrence was the man who began it. He had abandoned that ladder the moment the lights went out and made for the shipwrights' mess, on the port side, opposite the Sick Bay. The scuttles, or portholes, had light-excluding ventilators in place as a blackout precaution, but they were only plywood. Lawrence worked

away at one, to get it free; when an engineer officer came
to help him, he chased the man away to another port and
shouted to a bosun or bosun's mate, who came in just then,
to pass the word along.

Anyway, at that shout, there was a concerted rush from
the ladder, uphill into the shipwrights' mess. Blundell, on
the tail of the ladder line, was one of the first here, and
with another man he began to undo a ventilator. It was
held in place by butterfly nuts. As they worked at it, un-
screwing the nuts, the port was coming over above them,
and they were leaning backwards.

Bendell was still lying stunned on the inclined deck of
the Sick Bay. He came to, still dazed, to see a man with a
flashlight bending over him. It was Sick Berth Petty Officer Henry Main, checking that the Sick Bay was clear of
patients and staff. It was, except for Bendell. Main said,
"Get up, she's going," and, with his flashlight, led the way
to the door.

Neither could walk now, the list was too great. They
crawled up the deck, pulling themselves forward with their
hands. In the area outside, the flashlight was no longer
necessary. There was a wall of fire all along the starboard
battery and a man shouting that the boys' mess deck had
blown up. Directly below the battery, and above the A.A.
magazine, it was unlikely that anyone could now escape
from it.

On the port side they found a ladder leading to a hatch,
but the hatch was closed and they could not open it.
"We'll try the P.O.s' mess," said Main, and they crawled
on.

They now became separated, probably because Main
knew that mess and Bendell did not; instead, he somehow
blundered into the pantry next to it. He was now in pitch
darkness, alone, in a strange part of the ship, the only noise

being that of men shouting and trampling around, trying to get up ladders or tear open the ventilators.

After the second explosion, which seemed to him like two, Leading Signalman Fossey had logged the time. Then he looked round the flag-deck—it was now empty, except for Signalman Hutchins, his second hand, and the lights were out. He fumbled for the emergency signal lamps, but could not find them; they must have been shaken on to the deck somewhere.

He told Hutchins to go up on the compass bridge to see if he could switch on the masthead lights, then went himself into the signal house and telephoned the signal distributing office. Signalman Hudson answered. Fossey told him to clear the office and tell those in the W./T. office nearby that they were to make their way to the upper deck. Then he locked the box with the confidential books in it, and placed the key round his neck; shook awake Leading Signalman Harley, who was sleeping in the signal house; and told Hutchins, who had just returned unsuccessfully from the compass bridge, to get into the *Daisy II*.

As Hutchins left, another explosion occurred from aft and Fossey saw two sparks coming out abaft the funnel; he looked at the clock and logged the time—1:21. Then he heard Commander Nichols calling up from the boat deck, "Signalman, make a signal for assistance."

Fossey replied that he could not, as there were no lights working. Then he went back to the signal house, and found Harley still in bed. "For Christ's sake, turn out, Stripy," he protested, "the bloody ship's going to turn over." With that, the increasing list sent the heavy door of the signal house slamming shut on them—and they were trapped.

When the second explosion occurred and the battleship took on a heavy list, Commander Nichols was aware of what must happen, within minutes, as the sixty or so light-excluding but nonwatertight ventilators on the starboard side were submerged. But the failure of power, shown by the darkness below decks, in effect decapitated the executive officers. General orders could no longer be piped through the broadcast system and the Captain and Commander were reduced to purely local control in whatever part of the ship they happened to be at the time.

What Commander Nichols did was to give orders, as best he could to anyone in the vicinity, to cut free from their lashings all boats and Carley rafts, and anything else that would float. Having left his knife behind, he could not help with that, so went up onto "B" gun deck where the "church deals" were stowed; these were long wooden forms used for church parade. As Nichols climbed up, Lawrence burst open the light-excluding ventilator, to emerge on the ship's side; instead of walking down into the sea, he walked up to "B" gun deck and recognized Commander Nichols by his voice; all he could see of him was the blur of a white shirt. Together, they grabbed the ends of a "church deal" and, with a concerted swing, sent it clattering down the side into the water.

Just aft of "B" turret, two other men were trying to manhandle a Carley raft over the side. One was Leading Seaman E. A. Boxall, who had escaped from the boats' crews mess; the other, thought Boxall, was Lieutenant Commander Ward, but it was too dark to see properly. The drawback to the Carley raft was its weight and this one, normally needing five or six men, had to be carried up a steeply inclined deck and then maneuvered over the guardrails. It was an impossible task for just the two of them and, as no one else came to help, the officer said, "We can't do it on our own—so away you go." And Boxall went, jumping over the side, with the ship listing at about 45°.

Leading Supply Assistant Batterbury had just been blown up the ladder into the galley, in the superstructure below the gun deck. Here, he started groping around in the dark. "What are you looking for, chum?" someone asked. "Me cap," said Batterbury.

So firm was prewar naval discipline that the thought uppermost in his mind was that he could not go on deck without a cap. But, bareheaded, he left it and made his way up the heeling deck to the port guardrails. Sitting astride them, fully dressed, with his "brass hat" on, was a senior officer, he thought Admiral Blagrove, calling out an order to abandon ship to the men working at the Carley rafts and "church deals."

Batterbury climbed over the guardrails and walked down the side to the blister, a gigantic swelling from the side of the ship, which was now mostly out of the water. A sailor was sitting down on it, taking his shoes off. Batterbury thought that was sensible, and sat down to do the same. He got one shoe off, then lost his balance and, dressed only in thin undershirt and pants, went sliding on his back down the seaweed and barnacles towards the water. He felt no pain at the time and, despite the shock of the cold water and the burning in eyes and throat from its coating of fuel oil, was aware only of a feeling of relief. He was a strong swimmer, confident now that he would survive.

His messmate, Leading Supply Assistant Sims, a poor swimmer, had made for the picket boat, which was then still secured to the port boom forward. Sims ran out along the boom and dropped into her just as she was cut loose, her bow already rising out of the water.

It was Wilson who had given the order to cut. Coming out of the same galley as Sims and Batterbury, he had made for the port side, while most of the men with him melted

away to starboard. He slid over the side between the
two forward guns of the battery, then fell into black
space. It was a long way down, a long drop in darkness before he hit the bilge keel, which was already clear of the
water. In the tension of the moment he felt no pain, only
a jolt. He still held his flashlight in his hand.

He clambered out of the water into the picket boat
which, designed to take fifty-nine men, must now have had
over one hundred aboard, crammed into the forepeak, the
cabin aft, and on deck, with other men, in the water, holding on to her. So heavily was she laden that her sides,
amidships, were almost awash. Wilson thought it was time
to cut free. He was well-known, not for his rank, but as an
amateur ventriloquist popular at ship's concert parties.
Men would recognize his voice as that of a "Chiefy," and
obey. He and a midshipman began shouting orders and,
rocking under her terrible load, the bottom of the battleship coming up underneath her, the rope securing her to
the boom parted. But there was no power to move her, although Leading Stoker Boyle was down in the engine room,
trying to get steam up.

Wilson and the midshipman shouted orders for some
of the men to lie down in the gunwales and paddle at the
water with their hands. Slowly, very slowly, the picket boat
moved away from the heeling battleship. As she did so, a
man came hurtling down the side of the *Royal Oak*, struck
the rolling chocks (wooden stabilizers fitted to the underwater part of the hull), bounced off, fell into the water;
and came swimming fast for the picket boat. It was Leading Seaman Boxall, released from his duty of trying to free
the Carley raft. More and more men in the water began to
head for the picket boat.

It was not in fact due to Wilson's order that the picket
boat was now clear of the boom. Lieutenant Commander

Maclean, who had scrambled into her in full dinner dress, happened to have a small penknife in his pocket; after breaking one blade on the rope, he had now succeeded in severing it. Then he began to help swimmers on board; one of them, Lieutenant Commander Gregory, quickly took charge of the picket boat, but for a few minutes quite a number of people thought that it was they who were in command.

Up on "B" gun deck, Commander Nichols and Chief Stoker Lawrence had in quick succession thrown a dozen or so "church deals" down the side; at this moment, they had hold of another one. Lawrence recalls that there was now a final explosion, and that Nichols cried, "Good God, this is ours, come on!" Holding the ends of the plank, they ran and slid down towards the water. It was a little late. Nichols found the guardrail somehow above him, scrambled over, tried to walk, not down the side, but up it—for the ship was rolling over—and was then "quite gently" launched into the water. Lawrence, having dropped the "church deal," found water lapping at his feet, made a tremendous effort, and leaped out as far as he could. He went down into the water and recalls its phosphorescence; when he came up, he found that his right arm was useless and that he could not swim.

Bendell, too, remembers that final explosion and the great lurch of the ship which followed it. One moment, he had his feet in the sink of the pantry in the petty officers' mess, and was struggling to get out of the port. He could see the stars, but no land, through the port, for the land had now dropped below his level of vision. Then the whole compartment seemed to turn upside down, and he fell backwards into it in a shower of broken crockery; water poured in through the door, and a torrent came through the port. In a moment, he was up to his chin in water. But there the water stayed, just allowing him to breathe. There was an "air lock" in the flooded compartment.

Just a moment or two before, Fossey and Harley, trapped in the signal house by the slamming of the door, had managed to tear away the light-excluding ventilator on the starboard side; such was their desperation that Fossey nearly ripped off the top of one of his fingers. Harley, clad only in undershirt and pants, went through first, then helped Fossey who was fully dressed, with watch coat and sea boots on. They stood for a moment at the top of the ladder, with the sea coming up to them, as the ship rolled over. "Don't rush down, Stripy, stay where you are," said Fossey, and took a last glance into the signal house to look at the clock. He thought it registered 1:27.

Then the ship gave a terrific lurch to starboard. Up till then Fossey had somehow been convinced that the *Royal Oak* was too big to sink. Now he realized that she was done. "I think that was the first time I'd ever said my prayers, and meant it." He went over quick from the sponson deck, hitting his leg on something. Then, with a damaged leg, a finger nearly torn off, and fully dressed with sea boots on, he swam for his life away from the *Royal Oak*, which was coming over on top of him.

6

"The Whole Works Went Up"
(Amidships)

The main bulk of the *Royal Oak,* amidships, was taken up by the engine and boiler rooms, together with the Central Stores. Aft, under the batteries, were two stokers' mess decks connected by a cross-passage; forward of these were the communications mess and the boys' mess, on port and starboard sides respectively. Here, the first explosion in the bow had been vaguely heard and dimly felt. The second explosion occurred directly under the boys' mess deck, from which there were hardly any survivors; the third was directly below the stokers' mess; the last, after an interval, was aft again, under the Marines' mess deck.

Stoker Cleverley had got back into his hammock, just aft of the cross-passage. Above it was a perforated metal plate which carried the electric leads; Cleverley used it as a shelf for cigarettes and matches. He had almost got off to sleep again, when "the whole works went up." He was not backward in getting out of his hammock, but Leading Stoker Jones was faster still, perhaps because he was wide-awake after coming off duty. Jones covered the few feet between his hammock and the door in the after bulkhead.

Outside there was a ladder which led up into the lobbies by "X" barbette, from where it was possible to get out onto the quarter-deck. He was halfway up that ladder when the third explosion took place.

Cleverley, however, had only just jumped out of his hammock. As his feet hit the deck, it seemed to him that an explosion opened up the armored deck in the cross-passage leading to the port-side stokers' mess. The flash of it leaped out from there and struck men standing all around Cleverley; there was an appalling crash, and the lights went out.

Everything was black and red; everything burnable was smoldering, the hammocks glowing in the darkness. Cleverley, and about half a dozen other men, were on their feet; the rest of the stokers were huddled in the darkness where they had been thrown by the flash and blast. He could not understand why it was that they were dead or dying, and he still alive.

Unaware that the flash had burned him from the knees downwards, he reached for the box of matches on the carrier lead, but found that the matches would not strike. Then he shinned up a ladder into the starboard battery and, in the pitch darkness, lost himself.

Jones, already on the ladder at the third explosion, was shielded from the flash by the bulkhead; but, immediately afterwards, saw coming at him out of the dark from the direction of the Marines' mess deck aft, "a massive ball of orange flame." It was burning cordite, traveling in search of air too fast to run away from—he was in it for no more than a second, but instead of being on the ladder, he found himself flat on the deck. For some reason he did not then understand, he was unable to get up. When he did pull himself upright, the flame came traveling back, but this time did not throw him down.

He got up into the battery, turned to go forward, then heard, amid the crash of six-inch shells falling out of their racks with the heel of the ship, a shout of, "Keep going aft —everybody aft!" After that, he too lost sense of direction and began blundering about in the darkness. Protected only by a thin undershirt, he had severe cordite burns on legs, shoulders, arms, head and face—and was unaware of it.

Most of the men awakened from sleep wore only undershirt and shorts, apart from a wrist watch and a money belt. Only officers or petty officers normally wore pajamas. In the port-side stokers' mess deck hammocks caught fire, and as the sleeping men fell through them, they too began to blaze. Chief Stoker Philip Terry, who had told them all to dress at the first explosion, tried to beat out the flames on one stoker, and was badly burned about the hands in doing so. Another stoker, clad only in blazing underwear, was dashing around, calling out terribly. The last seen of him was as he ran into the worst of the fire.

Terry and Stoker William Campbell then dashed onto the boys' mess deck, where equally terrible sights met them. One of the boys' instructors, probably Petty Officer Nicolls, was trying to organize an orderly evacuation of the mess deck. It seems probable, too, that it was Petty Officer French and Able Seaman Judge who were then trying to help boys through the manhole in the main hatch. So few boys survived that accounts are fragmentary.

Both Terry and Campbell got through into the starboard battery and then up another ladder onto the upper deck; Terry made for the big power launch, going out along the boom towards it. Stoker Albert Bond tried a different route and made the upper deck by the forward A.A. guns on the port side. All three had been badly burned.

Less than thirty boys escaped from the *Royal Oak* and

most of these had been sleeping, not in the mess deck, but
in the three forward casemates of the starboard battery
directly above. Boy A. W. Scovell even went back for his
trousers but, in the darkness, could not find them. He
climbed up a ladder into the galley area, with a mass of
other boys; as they tried to open a door, water began to
come through it, so they swarmed up another ladder onto
the boat deck. For Boy G. L. Trewinnard the sinking of
the *Royal Oak* was merely the first adventure in a long
series when he was still very young—he was sunk in the following year off Norway, in the *Vandyke,* spent five years as
a prisoner of war and some time after that in Russia when
the Red Army came. He hardly remembers how he got
out of the *Royal Oak,* except that it was with his pal, Ernest
Upham. Scovell remembered very well how he felt, because he lost his footing on the boat deck—probably it was
smothered in oil flung up by the explosions—and went
straight into the drink.

This was directly by the starboard boom. The launch,
ordered away by Commander Nichols just after the first
explosion, was still secured to it. But, unlike the picket
boat, which was being pulled out of the water, the launch
was being forced under; the boat ropes were bar taut and
the end of the boom was jamming the launch.

Scovell tried to get into it, but both he and the launch
were by now too slippery with fuel oil; failing to get a grip,
he slid back into the water. Men in the launch were trying
to help swimmers on board and others were throwing out
gratings for them to cling to. Chief Stoker Terry, both arms
and hands badly burned, was struggling desperately to
clear the boat and get it away to save life. Then Stoker
Petty Officer Welch shouted to him, "Get clear, Chief, she's
coming over!"

Scovell had already gone, swimming away from the

bridge and tripod which was heeling over above them; at the last moment, Terry dived overboard and struck away. The spotting top hung for a moment above them all; then, as the ship rolled onto her starboard side, it fell in a sheet of spray, carrying the wreckage of the launch with it.

In the communications mess deck, opposite the Boys' mess, the second and third explosions did not cause a fire. Leading Telegraphist Raymond Jones leaped out in his underwear, leaving a fortnight's pay behind, and, with half a dozen of his messmates and a crowd of others, probably stokers, swarmed up the ladder into the port battery above. The lights had gone, but they could see, dimly and intermittently, by the flashes as an electric cable short-circuited.

One last ladder led to the upper deck. There was quite a scramble around it. "There was no panic or anything," said Jones, "it was just that there weren't many ways of getting up top. I suppose something like a thousand men had to funnel themselves onto the deck via about six gangways. It takes time, particularly in the small hours, when everyone has been woken from a deep sleep. There was a certain amount of jostling."

The final exit to the sea was through a heavy door in the narrow gallery which ran round the superstructure. Jones had a horrible feeling that he might not be able to open that door, but it was not secured and he emerged onto the upper deck, about ten yards from the port boom. The picket boat had already cast off, but he heard people shouting up around the gun turrets and saw figures silhouetted against the sky, apparently at work throwing Carley rafts over.

He had not stopped to think yet; but he did now, and decided—into the water, if possible. With the boom sticking up in the air at about 30°, he went over the guardrails

and slid down the side for about eight feet until he hit the
boom platform. He continued sliding, but was checked
again by the narrow ledge at the top of the blister. "So far,"
said Jones, "it was all paint work—comfortably smooth
sliding." After that, he went on to seaweed and barnacles
for quite a distance, until he hit the rolling strakes; the
wooden blocks held him for a moment during which he
looked beyond them and saw blackness—the surface of
the water. He seemed to be sliding all the time, and never
getting any nearer to it—which was partly true because, as
he went down, the side was coming further and further
out of the water, increasing the distance he had to travel.

From the rolling strakes downwards, he had no idea
what happened to him; he just found himself below the
surface, looking up through the water at the phosphores-
cent bubbles caused by his splash. Then he saw a Carley
raft bobbing about, and made for it. His watch, which he
still has, stopped finally and for good at 1:29.

Supply Petty Officer Finley had been standing, a deck
above Jones, outside the mail office just under the bridge;
he judged that the second explosion was directly opposite
him. "For me," he said, "this was my first *real* explosion.
There was a dash, and I kicked my shoes off, because
there'd be a swim for it." He ran to the ladder which led
up into the chief petty officers' and petty officers' recreation space, and had climbed it as far as the hatch coaming
when the third explosion seemed to hit directly below. It
was the same explosion which had blown the armored deck
in the cross-passage and cut down the stokers.

"From then," said Finley, "as it hit, I was hit. All I can
remember is a terrible flash and terrific heat." He flung up
his arms to protect his face and can remember falling.

He came to, lying under bits of broken wood, probably from the card tables in the recreation space. He could

feel the ship gradually heeling over. He shoved the bits
of wood away and put a hand to his head. "I found I'd no
hair left and the flesh was hanging in strips from my arms.
So something terrible had crashed me. I didn't worry about
that, then—my sole intention was to get out as quick as
I could."

He saw another man there, and, in the dim light, linked
hands with him. There was a stink of cordite, or something similar. Someone said, "Strike a match." The two men
stumbled out into a cross-passage and went through another door into the wardroom. As they stumbled down the
slope of the deck, Finley lost the other man. He came to a
door, looked out, saw the water—and a six-inch gun
pointed down at an angle of 20° to 30°. Finley thought,
"Thank God!" and dived in.

Stoker Oswald Fletcher cannot have been far from Finley, for he was caught by the flash outside the police office,
then followed him up the ladder and into the wardroom,
burned on his legs and face. By that time there were about
thirty men trying to get out of the wardroom, dashing
round in the dark and being pinned and crushed by the
furniture as it broke loose with the increasing heel of the
ship. Fletcher was lucky, for his groping fingers found a
light-excluding ventilator, which he unscrewed and pulled
out. When he climbed through the port, he found that the
water was almost up to it.

Other men, pouring up from the stokers' mess deck into
the darkened after part of the battery—the forward part
was on fire—had blundered into the lobbies under the
wardroom. Jones was in pitch darkness until someone
pulled aside the hessian blackout curtain obscuring the
screen door onto the quarter-deck; the gray darkness of the
night had a different quality, and he stumbled towards it.
Once outside, he was walking in water, and must have

passed quite close to where Paymaster Commander Cundall was lying helpless by the guardrails. Cleverley was
stumbling about blind in what he knows now, but did not
know then, was the gunroom. But he felt cold air, and
knew what that meant—a light-excluding ventilator. "I was
in a bit of a panic, because the ship was on her beam
ends, nearly." He then performed the incredible feat of
diving straight through the ventilator, taking it with him;
he was in the water at once, for the quarter-deck was under. When he looked up, he saw "X" turret above him.
"Then I broke all records for thirty yards, because the ship
was coming over."

Opposite these lobbies, on the port side of the ship, were
the "heads," where the long line had been assembled and,
nearby, the divisional office, where Petty Officers Kerr and
Puddy had been standing. Both were knocked flat by the
second explosion. The bulkheads moved and shook. Dommett, seeing to his horror an orange pillar of cordite flame
come leaping up the hatch by the "heads," tried to outrun
it. He was knocked flat on his face, but got to hands and
knees in time to see the flame destroy the double curtains of
the screen door and vanish out onto the quarter-deck, leaving behind blazing fragments which burned him as he staggered after it. Quite dazed, he stumbled along the rails,
well past where the *Daisy* was lying, the thought uppermost in his mind being that he had promised to tell his
friends what had happened. Gradually, as the ship heeled
over, he realized that he never would get back to the mess.
He knew that his hair had been burned off, but was not yet
aware of any other injuries.

Instance and Hearn were in the "heads" when they
heard an explosion, either the second or the third. Both
turned away and made for the entrance, not yet really
alarmed. On that, there was a double bang aft, a blast of

hot air, and a bright orange flame hit both men, hurling them back inside the "heads." For what seemed an eternity, the blazing cordite roared round and round the narrow space. The pain was excruciating.

Instance had put on thick trousers and a jersey, which protected his body; but there was no protection for his head and hands. He buried his face in his hands, then the pain at the back of his neck was so terrible that he clasped that instead. But the flame scorching at his face made him clap his hands over his eyes. To breathe was death. It was a question of how long he could endure the agony and still hold his breath.

Then the flame was gone. After that glare, the darkness was impenetrable. Instance found himself on hands and knees, unable to stand—why, he did not know. He began to pull himself forward and, just outside the door, crawled over the body of a man. The corpse was wearing only undershirt and pants—"he must have gone up like a match," said Instance.

He had no idea what had happened to Hearn and Hancock, who had been next to him in the line; he next saw them, covered to the eyes in bandages, in hospital. "All I knew was, that I was singed, and that I wanted fresh air; I wanted to get out." He began to crawl in the pitch darkness towards a cross-passage which would lead eventually to the starboard screen door. He knew there were hatches ahead of him, and that he might fall down them. He could see nothing whatever, he was guided only by his knowledge of the ship.

Meanwhile, Kerr and Puddy had picked themselves up, coughing violently from cordite gas in the lungs. By the divisional office there was no fire yet, but the second explosion had blown down the hessian curtains at the officers' bathroom—and that was their escape route to a door which led into the port battery. "Here you are, lads, in here!" called out Kerr.

After him dashed Puddy, Marine Sandford, and another man he did not recognize in the dark. "It wasn't dark for long," Kerr said, in an account written shortly afterwards. "Fire seemed to be eating the air and we were all coughing." Sandford tried to open the door leading to the battery, then ran, shouting, "We're done, it's stuck." Sandford did find an alternative route, got over to the port side, and died there.

Kerr stuck to the door, but the list of the ship had wedged the handles inside the framework. Through the cracks in the door Kerr could see there was an inferno beyond, the handles were getting too hot to touch; but behind them there was no retreat, the fire was at their backs. In desperation Kerr, who is a big, heavy man, began to kick at the door. When it seemed he must suffocate with the fumes, it gave, and Kerr shouted, "Come on, lads, it's opened!"

But there was no sign of anyone near him now, there were only sounds. Men were coughing and somebody was running around in a bad way, calling out, "Oh, oh!" And from somewhere in the starboard casemates there was a terrible screaming.

The worst was still ahead of him. He flinched back from the red flames outside, then forced himself to run deliberately into them. There was no other escape. For a moment, he staggered and nearly fell, his legs seeming to fold under him helplessly. Then he was through, blundering about and clutching out for support. He pulled himself along by a hammock, then fell over something. His hands caught hold of guardrails and a chain—and he knew then that he was at the hatch outside the "heads." The port-side screen door was not far away.

As he made for it, an explosion came up the hatch he had just left—but it seemed to blow forward and miss him. There was nothing to stop him now, the cordite flame had dissolved the hessian curtains, and he could see where the "black night" was. Minutes after Dommett, he made the quarter-deck, and the fresh air seemed to revive him.

Instance was still traveling on hands and knees through the darkened cross-passage inside the ship. When he came to a turning into the starboard screen passage, despite his dreadful injuries, he knew where he was. He had served before in this class of ship, and knew them blindfold; otherwise he never would have got out.

After pulling himself thirty feet along the screen passage, he came to the hessian curtain. Normally there would have been an armored door, clipped down. Now there was only the curtain to drag aside. He pulled it back, and looked out onto the quarter-deck.

It was heeled over at an angle of 45°. He had not been crawling along the deck at all for that last thirty feet, but on the bulkhead. It was, too, the first indication he had that the ship was sinking.

Instance pulled himself up by the framework of the door, stepped out onto the quarter-deck—and felt his legs go from under him. He skidded down the deck, cracked open the right side of his head on some projection, and arrived in a heap at the starboard guardrails. Standing there, telescope under his arm, the water pouring onto the deck and up over his feet, was a midshipman. It was probably the midshipman of the watch. "Do you think we should abandon ship?" said the boy.

As he spoke, the battleship lurched heavily, the guardrails went right under, and they both floated off into the icy sea.

7

"Who Knocked the Handle off That Cup?"

(Aft)

The Marines' mess deck lay around the barbette of "Y" turret, separating the crew's quarters from the officers' cabin area; it stretched right across the ship, with the barbette roughly in the center. Directly above was the quarter-deck. Right forward of the mess, in a cross-passage, was a ladder at the top of which was a sliding armored shield. To starboard, forward, there was a way out which led into the battery on that side. Aft, there were heavy watertight doors in the bulkhead, one port and one starboard, which led into the cabin area and so to a ladder to the quarter-deck.

At 1:16 the mess deck was an orderly array of mess tables and hammocks, with most of the men turned in. A moment later, it was a blazing shambles.

Sergeant Parham, the gunnery instructor, was just finishing his cigarette. Near him some Marines were standing by the hammock netting. He heard two explosions and saw a flame go in among the Marines, cutting them all down. He himself was only "singed," so he ran into the mess deck and tried to wake people who were seemingly still asleep

78

in their hammocks. He shook Corporal E. W. Cunningham, who did not stir, then ran to the watertight door leading to the cabin area on the port side. He began to knock off the clips, to open it, but was hampered by a crowd of about twenty men, all trying to get at it; the last clip on the left would not move because people were already pulling at the door. By now the whole mess deck was shuddering—probably it was the shaking of the ship as enormous masses of water boiled into her engine rooms and poured onto the decks as the light-excluding ventilators slowly went under with the increasing heel; Parham thought it meant she was going any moment.

Saltmarsh's hammock had collapsed, and he went sprawling on the deck by the barbette. Barry Hawes found his hammock on fire, and leaped out. Stanley Rowlands ran for the way out into the starboard battery, found sounds of pandemonium coming from there—and the door jammed. He wasted no time at it—"you only had seconds in which to operate"—but ran back to the mess deck.

Sergeant Booth, looking forward, saw a flame come along the port lower passage—and fell back out of the way. "The next thing I remember is seeing hammocks ablaze, mess tables burning, and crockery falling off them—a cup on the deck was rolling backwards and forwards. I remember thinking, 'Who knocked the handle off that cup?' I got to my feet and wondered why I was slipping—then I realized the ship was listing. As the flame hit one man, I saw a look of intense fright and pain come onto his face, then the flesh just curled off, like paper off a wall. There was a sudden smell, of pork cooking and burning wool. As he fell towards me, I gripped him by the arm—a piece of flesh came off, showing bone underneath. He fell on the deck a yard away from me, moaning. Everyone seemed to be shouting and screaming. Men were on their hands and

knees, calling out for their mothers, in the knowledge they
were mortally wounded. Others were crying in agony,
'F——g roll on!' Flesh was hanging off some of them."

On the starboard side, men were falling in flames out of
their hammocks, and seeming to fall into flames, as if the
deck below the hammocks had collapsed. The whole starboard side of the mess deck seemed to be melting and cav-
ing in. Barry Hawes, leaping from his burning hammock,
dodged round it, and saw that the starboard watertight
door, aft, unlike the port door, was slightly ajar. He ran
straight through in his underwear and into the officers'
quarters, and did not see what happened after that. Marine Owens was through it on his heels, with the cries of
burning men in his ears; he does not want to remember.

Sergeant Booth saw a man's hammock burning, with the
man lying silently in it; he ran his hands up it, to put out
the flames. The man fell out, onto the deck, and lay there,
dead, or past hope. Another man was jammed up in his
hammock, with the cap box hooks driven into his body.
When Booth tried to release him, he remained inert and
silent.

When the third explosion occurred, some quarter of a
minute or more after the second, a searing flash, coming
from forward, went right round the mess deck and a huge
belch of flame roared up apparently through the deck on
the starboard side. At that moment Sergeant Parham,
struggling to get the last clip off the watertight door, finally
succeeded. Men poured through it, flinging back the heavy
steel door and pinning him against the bulkhead. The
lights went out, and the mess was left in a glowing darkness, the flames obscured by the smoke.

So far, the N.C.O.s had managed to keep some sort of
order. Saltmarsh, who was very young at the time, recalled
one older man, experienced in world war one, to whom

they all looked up. He forgot the name, but can remember him shouting orders in succession to cope with each factor, until the situation went finally beyond all human control. When the first flame swept in, he had shouted, "Come on, get those hoses reeled off!" Saltmarsh had run to obey. Then, when it was clear the fire could not be fought, he ordered him to open the port-side watertight door, which had now slammed shut. "This voice," said Saltmarsh afterwards, "this one man, instilling sense into men just standing there, gawking. He was slapping 'em, chivvying 'em, goading 'em on."

It was probably Sergeant McLaverty, a first world war man, who did admit to forcibly getting Priestley, the fifteen-year-old bugler, out of his hammock, slapping him round the ears, and telling him to get on deck. In the reeking chaos of the heeling mess deck, dimly seen, other N.C.O.s were giving up their own chances of escape. Corporal H. D. Jordan, an enthusiastic Rover Scout, kept a way open for other men to get through. Saltmarsh saw him, and thought it was a hatch he was holding open; McLaverty's recollection is that it was a watertight door. At the last, he told Jordan to look after himself, and Jordan replied, "No, Sergeant Mac, not till they're through." But he was dead before that, shriveled by the flames. Corporal Marsh died in the same way, in the boat-hoist area, hands over his face to protect them from the flames, as he saw the younger Marines through.

"Cats" Cunningham was the Corporal of Saltmarsh's mess. Noted for his scruffiness, he would stand up to the Color Sergeant on behalf of a Marine, if he thought the latter was in the right. In Saltmarsh's opinion, he was worth "two and a half ordinary corporals." Saltmarsh was suddenly called away from trying to open the watertight door by a shout from Marine Tuckwood, "Give a hand

over here!" With Jimmy Woods, he ran over, to find Tuckwood supporting Cunningham, dreadfully burned about
the head. At that moment the fourth explosion occurred,
almost under the starboard side of the mess deck, where
they were, and the whole pattern, of one man helping another, disintegrated.

Previously, the deck covering may have been on fire
giving the impression that the deck had itself collapsed;
after this explosion, there was no further doubt about it.
Stanley Rowlands, who had just doubled back from his
fruitless attempt to get out into the battery, hung there ap-
palled. His way aft was blocked by an enormous hole in
the plating, belching smoke and flame. The ship lurched
heavily, and Saltmarsh, losing his footing, fell down the incline towards the flaming gap. Other men, too, were rolling down towards it, then vanishing into the fires below.
As Saltmarsh slid helplessly, he hit an obstruction—the
coaming of a small hatch leading below to the fan space—
and there he hung for a moment.

At that instant, Sergeant Booth had been going up the
ladder forward of the barbette, on the heels of two Marines. He had been helping men to get up through the sliding armored hatch above, but had now judged it was time
he looked after himself. The explosion and the lurch which
followed unleashed the sliding armored shield. Like a
crude guillotine it slid easily on its runners, as it was designed to do; with massive power it slammed across the
gap and caught the two nearly naked men squarely at
the waist. What was left, the bloody lower halves of two
bodies, fell back down the ladder on to Booth; and the
three of them, the two half corpses and the one live man,
thudded to the heeling deck.

As he hit, Booth grasped at the chain around the bottom of the ladder and hung on, to stop himself from slid-

ing down the deck towards the starboard side. "Down there," he said, "it didn't look like a mess deck any more—there were fountains of water coming in—I couldn't understand how it got there—there were no tables visible, just oil —I could smell that—with things floating on it and flames blazing. And I thought, 'Now, how am I going to get out?'"

Rowlands, right over on the starboard side, with the door to the battery jammed behind him and the deck opened up ahead, paused for a moment. "The whole of the starboard mess deck had gone;" he said, "I think the bowels were out of the ship. And water was absolutely pouring into her." The water must already have been lapping over the quarter-deck above him, it was forcing its way through the light-excluding ventilators in a torrent.

"I couldn't describe it," he said. "Where hammocks had been, there wasn't anything. I saw a couple of Marines in flames—I didn't know if they were dead yet—they were lying at the far end of the mess deck. I got aft by crawling along where the deck is re-inforced to the bulkhead." With his shoulder pressed to the side of the ship and his feet on that narrow ledge above the gap, he inched his way along towards the after watertight door.

On the opposite side, Booth also was going aft, holding on to stop himself sliding. Saltmarsh was climbing up the deck on hands and knees, away from the inferno on the starboard side. Reaching the port side and using a mess table as a bench, he tried to open a port. Another man, he thought it was Marine Ellis, came to help him undo the cleats of the deadlight. When they freed it, "it came down with a terrific whack and knocked somebody else off his hold. I didn't wait on that, but climbed through the porthole and sat down on the side of the ship." The man Saltmarsh thought was Ellis came through after him, then said sharply, "I'm going back for me money," and disappeared.

Sergeant McLaverty, giving no thought to his German Mae West, got out by going forward under the port battery, where for a moment he saw Marine F. W. C. Sandford. Sandford had been in the officers' bathroom with Petty Officer Kerr, but had left when he found the door to the port battery jammed. He must have found an alternative route, for he was now coming towards McLaverty, shouting, "Beggar this for civvy street!" Beneath him, the deck seemed to buckling, and he vanished in the smoke. McLaverty found a ladder forward and went up it, "in a blast of hot air, I didn't get my feet on the rungs." Once on the quarter-deck, he had to put his foot on "X" barbette to get enough push to reach the guardrails.

Below, from the ruined mess deck, the first rush of Marines had already poured aft into the officers' cabin area. One of their officers, Lieutenant Benton, slept on the starboard side a few feet from the watertight door. When the second explosion occurred, he stopped listening for airplanes, leaped out of his bunk, and made straight for the door, in order to find out what was happening on the mess deck. Then there was a third explosion and a red glow coming at him; the watertight door slammed in his face, and the flame never reached him. He turned and ran aft, where he met the dentist, Surgeon Lieutenant Dickie, the officer who had taken a third light from Keen's match. Benton was in pajamas, Dickie in dinner dress. Rather white-faced, they asked each other what had happened. Then ten Marines, in various stages of undress, came running aft, and began to ask them the same question. There was a ladder nearby, leading to the quarter-deck, but it had a black hessian curtain around it. Perhaps they were subconsciously afraid of being caught in the curtain, but none of them made any attempt to get up it. The ship took on a noticeable list, the lights dimmed down and went out, and the fans ran down with a whining noise.

"This way!" yelled Benton, and ran for the only sliding door which was open; it led into the Admiral's pantry. He had to climb across a piece of furniture which had slid across the door, then jump down in bare feet onto a deck covered with broken crockery. He scrambled up onto the sink, beating about with his hands to find the port which he thought would be there. Then his hands, slapping steel, produced a hollow boom from a wooden light-excluding ventilator, and he set to work on the butterfly nuts holding it in place. They were hard to move

He was surprised that the men behind him were so patient, there were no cries of "Hurry up!" It was so quiet that he could actually hear the water pouring in through the submerged light-excluding ventilators on the starboard side. That made him hurry. The ventilator came away in his hands, and he slung it, wondering if he would be, after all that, too large a man to get through.

Barry Hawes, standing silent immediately behind him, was wondering exactly the same thing. "I saw Benton's stern as he started to climb out—I wished he'd hurry up, and I wondered how long he'd take. Then, instead of diving into the sea, as I expected, he turned and crawled up on top. When I went through, I saw why—the ship was right over and you couldn't drop into the water, you'd have gone rolling down the port side."

Owens, too, went straight past the ladder and on into the pantry, where he saw a midshipman in pajamas; he could also see gray sky through the port, and went right through it, followed by the midshipman. Together they began to walk down the port side, the ship had heeled so much in that short time that it was now negotiable.

A rather hopeless little group were standing—or, rather, trying to keep their balance—in pitch darkness around the curtained ladder to the quarter-deck. Marine Moore, with one arm badly burned, had gone there after going through the port watertight door opened by Parham. Rowlands was the last to arrive, having inched his way past the gaping inferno in the mess deck. After the glare of the flames, he could see nothing. Men were hammering at the hatch above, but even the manhole was battened down; in that darkness, they had little or no chance of opening it. "It was very quiet," said Rowlands, "no one made much noise; you could hear the water coming in. I said my prayers."

Then someone else arrived, there was a splutter of a match, and they could see what they were doing; in a moment, the manhole was opened and they poured onto the quarter-deck. They struggled forward to the gangway, holding onto the guardrails.

Below, Sergeant Booth was lying across a ladder. It should have been upright, but must by now have been nearly horizontal, he could feel it in his back. He could remember making his way aft as far as the watertight door leading to the cabin area. It had been blocked by a wash-deck locker which had fallen over. He had got on top of that, then jumped. The list of the ship must have confused him, for he had struck his head violently on something. Now dazed, in pitch darkness, he was beginning to feel frightened. "Then," he said, "tremendous waves of noise beat in my ears—it was just as if I was tied to the clapper of a bell. And that's the last thing I remember of the *Royal Oak*."

8

"Every Time a Coconut"

(Quarter-deck)

When the second explosion occurred followed, he thought, by two others in quick succession, Engineer Commander Renshaw was still superintending the opening of the capstan area. The place filled immediately with dense smoke and the ship heeled over rapidly. There was obviously no chance of the Chief Stoker's escaping from the trunk, the Captain had gone up the ladder to the forecastle, followed by the others, and Renshaw himself was nearly asphyxiated by the fumes. He, too, stumbled up onto the forecastle, where it was so dark that he could see nothing. Taking his flashlight out of his pocket, he made his way aft along the port side, his eyes gradually becoming accustomed to the gloom. As he came to "B" turret, he could see men going over the boom into the picket boat; it was obviously going to be overcrowded and, he thought, no place for him.

At this point, or very shortly afterwards, there was a great splash from the starboard side, as the spotting top carried away from the heeling tripod and fell into the sea. When Renshaw reached the quarter-deck he met Admiral

Blagrove, who said, "What caused those explosions, Engineer Commander?"

"Torpedoes, sir," said Renshaw, who could think of no other cause.

"Good God!" replied Blagrove, in a tone of very great surprise.

The Admiral then went forward along the port side towards the bridge, the heel then being so great that Renshaw had to hold on to the guardrails. It seems certain that Batterbury was not mistaken when he recalled seeing the Admiral sitting on the guardrails near the bridge, calling out, "Every man for himself," or words to that effect. After that point, what happened to Admiral Blagrove seems to be hearsay, based on uncertain identifications in dim light.

A very short time only had now elapsed since the second explosion, it may have been less than five minutes. On the starboard side, the launch had gone, apparently crushed by the spotting top; from the starboard scuppers, Cundall and Instance, lying burned, had floated off; when Jones and Cleverley followed them out of the screen door, the whole starboard side of the quarter-deck was already under water.

Keen, Pirie, Owen and other junior officers were trying to unship the gig, right aft on the quarter-deck. Looking forward, Owen could see flames in the port battery and men coming out through them onto the quarter-deck. Kerr more or less fell through the screen door, the skin burned completely away from his head and hands—he bears the "tidemarks" of the inferno to this day. The fresh air revived him, and he went uphill to the guardrails and joined in an effort to get men down into the *Daisy II*. Contrary to what was generally believed by survivors, one man only stepped "dry" into the drifter, and he was not an officer.

According to Skipper Gatt, this man seemed dazed and did not know how he had got there. Almost certainly it was Musician John Thompson, who afterwards told Kerr that he had been burned outside the "heads," and had gone straight down into the drifter from the quarter-deck. There were two reasons why no one else got into the *Daisy*, the first of them being that she was secured, not at the port accommodation ladder, but forward of it, leaving the gangway clear for boats to come alongside.

When the second explosion occurred, Skipper Gatt told the cook, the only other man on deck, to cut the head rope; he himself ran to the wheelhouse to ring for "full astern." The cook shouted out, "I haven't got my knife!" so Gatt told him to throw the rope off the bollard. By then it was too late, the battleship's port blister, coming out of the water, was rising up underneath the *Daisy*, there was a dreadful grinding noise, and the drifter heeled over, tautening the head ropes so much that it was impossible to free them from the bollards. The battleship was then heeling one way with the drifter, caught on the blister, heeling the other; the stern of the *Daisy* was almost awash but her bows were twenty-five feet out of the water, locked by her bilges on to the *Royal Oak*'s blister. The grinding noises continued.

While this was happening Kerr saw a midshipman and an officer, who, he thought, was Lieutenant Commander Cook, trying to help men get down a rope into the heeling drifter; he himself went to another rope and, in spite of his burned hands, helped men to climb down it. But the port side was rising out of the water and the drop was becoming longer every moment; the *Daisy* was heeling over, and the gap between her side and the quarter-deck was steadily increasing. With her engine at "full astern," in an effort to pull loose from the blister, water was frothing around the stern of the drifter; men were jumping from the

quarter-deck, bouncing off the side of the battleship, and
falling into this turmoil. There was a cry from the quarter-
deck "*Daisy*, stop your engines!" An officer, standing on
the quarter-deck, cast off her stern rope; it fell into the
water, and wrapped itself round her screw.

An obvious way down to the water was by the accommodation ladder. Keen afterwards heard that Acting Lieutenant Vincent, the very junior Marine officer on duty,
had marshaled an orderly file of men to go down it. As the
ship listed, he stood there, shouting "Roll, bowl, or pitch,
every time a coconut, form queue here, my lucky lads!"
But as the ship heeled over, the gangway rose higher and
higher out of the water. Dommett, dazed from his burns,
had been one of the first to go down it; from right down at
the bottom of the ladder, he could see clearly what was
happening. Men were jumping off all around him, but
they were either hitting the battleship's port propeller
shafts, now clear of the sea, or falling into the water boil-
ing astern of the *Daisy*'s screw. He forced his way up the
gangway, to try to stop any more men coming down the
ladder and, with the aid of Surgeon Lieutenant E. D.
Caldwell, succeeded. Then, with a roar, the *Daisy* slid off
the blister, the head ropes having already parted with the
strain, and Gatt immediately stopped his engine.

He handed a life buoy to a deck hand, but the man
gave it back, saying "No, you're a married man, I'm single."

At this moment Benton, having got onto the quarter-
deck from the Admiral's pantry, made his way with diffi-
culty to the head of the accommodation ladder. Captain
Edgar Balls, the senior Marine officer, was by the guardrails. Benton did not know then that he could not swim,
but noticed only that he seemed very quiet. The *Daisy* had
just gone astern out of it, and there were, Benton thought,

at least thirty men left behind on the accommodation ladder, discussing the matter. "Discussing," said Benton, "was perhaps not quite the right word for it, but no one had yet given any command to abandon ship and the majority verdict seemed to be, 'Don't go yet—wait for the order.'"

Then the hatch on the quarter-deck opened and a small group, Rowlands and Moore among them, burst out. Rowlands saw a warrant officer sitting down at the top of the accommodation ladder and crying like a child. Alarmed at the heel of the ship, he yelled, "Come on, let's get out of it!" Engineer Commander Renshaw took off his shoes, went over the guardrails, and started to walk down the side. Able Seaman Farley, who had got out forward, was walking along the side towards the *Daisy*, hoping to get into her. Saltmarsh was sitting on the side, wondering what to do. There was an explosion, somewhere under the quarter-deck, and the ship gave a sudden lurch. Lieutenant Keen, heaving away at the starboard side of the gig, lost his balance, slipped, and went skidding down the deck into the sea. The gig came free, slid across the deck, and jammed up against a ventilator. "At this point," said Cadet Owen, "I thought that was enough of that, and I went through the port guardrails."

Midshipman Pirie thought the same, and jumped outwards from the stern; so did Lieutenant Henry Duncan and Barry Hawes, who just cleared the blister. Men were jumping and sliding down the port side, as it rolled up under their feet, tearing themselves open on the razor-like barnacles. Benton found it easy; the barnacles gave a grip to his bare feet. Keeping his balance, he ran down the side, saw a propeller shaft in front of him, thought, "Shall I go over or under?"—and took a leap clean over it. Lieutenant Sclater slid under the shaft, cutting himself badly on the barnacles.

Dommett was hanging on to the port guardrails, watching "X" and "Y" turrets cast loose. Of their own accord, the guns slowly swung round and pointed their muzzles down at the water. Instance, swimming along the starboard side of the quarter-deck and still dazed by his burns, saw two fifteen-inch gun muzzles looking down at him, and thought it might be an hallucination.

At the lurch, the men holding on to ropes on the port side let go their hold; Kerr dropped the end of his rope and got outboard of the guardrails, which were now horizontal. Then he took off his jacket and trousers and laid them across the rails, thinking as he did so of the current silly song, "Hanging Up the Washing on the Siegfried Line." He also mentally noted that he was going to lose the 14s. in silver in the trousers pockets, then got hold of the fender rope, to prevent himself from slipping. When he got into the sea, he kicked off so violently that he sprained his foot. A few yards away, Parham did the same thing with a wire holding the accommodation ladder. Rowlands never made the port guardrails at all, he went sliding backwards across the quarter-deck into the sea.

The ship gave another lurch, as still more bulkheads gave way, and like a great whale, she rolled right over and stood on her fighting top. Engineer Commander Renshaw, having taken two steps down the side, was thrown over backwards into the sea. At that moment, Able Seaman Farley, running along the side towards where Renshaw was, was also thrown backwards over the quarter-deck. As he fell through the air, he had visions of hitting a turret or ventilator and suffering broken bones which, in the circumstances, would be the undoubted end of him. But nothing interrupted his fall, and he went down deep into water black with oil.

Five or six men came swimming away in a ragged line

from the port side, singing, "Roll Out the Barrel"; among them were Batterbury and a Marine, a senior N.C.O., with a greatcoat on. As he began to weaken, there were shouts of, "Hang on, Stripy." From the stern another group, in which was Barry Hawes, plunged in and struck out, singing like mad, "Run, Rabbit, Run," so pleased were they to have escaped. It was involuntary and quite spontaneous. Few looked back, they were all too intent on getting away from her, for fear of suction or an explosion in the magazines.

But Leading Stoker Jones, well clear on her starboard side, saw a man running along the hull towards the stern; and Sims, who had been thrown off the picket boat, saw an explosion aft as she began the final lurch. Instance, close under her starboard side, and making away diagonally towards the stern, saw the ship in the dim light falling over towards him, and was conscious of the boats and gear which might carry away. "The thing which struck me most," he said, "was the tremendous noise; it was like a huge tin, full of nuts and bolts, slowly turning over. Racks of shells must have been coming loose, and other gear, so that anybody still inside had no hope. It must have been an absolute nightmare." Midshipman Pirie, holding on to a piece of wood astern of the battleship, saw her port propeller shafts clear of the water, then he saw her rudder appear and finally, as she rolled right over, one of her starboard screws. Inside her still were nearly eight hundred men.

Sergeant Booth never knew how he got out. His last memory was of lying across a ladder and then of a tremendous ringing noise in his ears. He came to, in the water, stark naked and clutching the cigarette lighter which his wife had sent him the previous day. It seems he can only have been blown out of the ship by that final explosion, which may have been a small-caliber magazine detonating.

Sick Berth Attendant Bendell was equally confused. One moment he had been attempting to get through the porthole in the pantry of the petty officers' mess, then "there was another bang, everything seemed to go upside down, and I fell back into the compartment. There was a clatter as pots and pans fell, too, and at the same time water came in at the port. Then, perhaps because the door had closed with the increasing heel of the ship, a bubble of air was trapped in the pantry. I don't really know what happened, or how it happened, but I had my head in air. Not much of it, I was touching the deckhead with my head. I think water had come in through the porthole, and that the ship was either on the bottom or completely upside down, with the starboard upper portholes submerged." It was not the deckhead, but the deck, which he was touching with his head, for the ship was capsized; the air lock must have formed on one side of the compartment, because the *Royal Oak*'s starboard side was nearer the sea bed than the port side. The only exit now was the open porthole, some five feet down through the dark, oil-smeared water.

The surface of Scapa Flow was some forty or fifty feet above him, and the bottom of the *Royal Oak* was still visible. At least half a dozen men were still on the capsized hull. Marine Moore was one of them. Two of the boys, Trewinnard and Upham, were there; Trewinnard was taking his trousers off, in anticipation of a swim. The Navigator, Lieutenant Commander Gregory, was walking up and down with a stoker, smoking. One of them had a pack of cigarettes, the other a box of matches, so they had lit up. He could hear air and gobs of fuel oil gurgling up around the hull, but it was too dark to see anything; he thought, however, that her upperworks were already on the bottom

and that she might not go down much further. But if he
was wrong, he risked being sucked down with her. Gregory
was determined not to leave one minute before it was absolutely necessary. He did not fancy his chances in the
bitterly cold water, and each minute spent out of it was
one minute more of life. When Gregory felt it was time at
last to go, he threw down his cigarette—and automatically
made to stamp it out; he looked at his watch—it showed
1:33; then, with the stoker, he waded off the hull into the
water, as if from a beach.

Fifty feet down, in the flooded compartment, Bendell
had gone underwater and was fumbling around as if
blindfolded for the porthole. He failed, and surfaced in
the air lock, gasping for breath. Then he took another gulp
of air and went down again. He beat about frantically, but
could not find the port, so floundered up towards the air
lock. It wasn't there. Either it had gone, or he had lost his
sense of direction. "Now I've had it," he thought, and took
a few mouthfuls of water, to end it quick.

The water must have been contaminated with fuel oil,
for it made him sick. Writhing, he spat it out. Then, with
no memory of finding the porthole, or even of going
through it, he was shooting up towards the surface; lucky
for him that he had exhausted the air in his lungs, or they
might have burst when he reached the surface.

All that was left of the battleship now was a dark hump
on the black water; from the swaying, laden picket boat,
Chief Engine-room Artificer Wilson thought it looked like a
football stadium, with froth bubbling around the sides.
Leading Seaman Boxall, also from the picket boat, saw
flickering lights from bow to stern, as if she was a furnace
inside and some of the plates had started; Leading Seaman
Instance, from the opposite side of the wreck, saw blue
flashes, as if generators were being earthed; Supply Petty

Officer Finley saw them, too. Marine Hawes thought she looked like a big whale. To Skipper Gatt, nursing the leaking *Daisy II*, she was a menace, a submerged obstruction beneath the oil-smeared water.

Slowly she went from sight, carrying down eight hundred living men, until her mainmast and fighting top struck the sea bed and the whole 29,000 tons of her forced them like spears into the sand; she settled slightly on her starboard side, the muzzles of the fifteen-inch guns being forced up to full elevation. Gatt knew she could not be far down and that low water would probably reveal her. From the sunken hull, oil poured up in an endless stream, fouling the water in great, spreading waves many feet thick. And from somewhere near the sunken bow, Sick Berth Attendant Bendell scraped up the port side and broke surface, the last man alive out of the *Royal Oak*.

9

"Daisy, Daisy, Give Me Your Answer, Do"

On the water now were only two boats, the picket boat, which had no power, and the *Daisy*, with a rope wrapped round her screw. The liberty launch, tied to the starboard boom, and capable of holding hundreds of men, had gone —shattered by the spotting top as the battleship rolled over. The gig, with the cover still on it, had floated off the quarter-deck and was now drifting astern, water-logged. There was one Carley raft complete—just one—and buckled parts of other Carley rafts, probably those damaged in the gale and stacked on the forecastle. There were a number of "church deals," including those thrown down the side by Commander Nichols and Chief Stoker Lawrence; there were gratings thrown out from the launch; and the crew of the drifter were now throwing overboard anything that would float—life belts, gratings, bits of wood.

The water temperature was 48° F. In theory, the extreme limit of life for a man in the water, or floating in a Carley raft in contact with the water, would be two hours;

but an hour would be more reasonable.* Out of the water, there was a biting wind which would kill just as quickly. Additionally, many of the swimmers were badly burned or bleeding from barnacle cuts.

The nearest land was half a mile away, it consisted of rocks backed by high cliffs; the nearest road was two-thirds of a mile inland from the cliffs, and there were hardly any dwellings, merely a few farmhouses. The Flow was utterly dark, no one saw any northern lights; nothing stirred and no alarm was given. Skipper Gatt began to signal "S O S, S O S, S O S, S O S, S O S," on the drifter's whistle, but there was no reaction. The main fleet anchorage was empty and the ships off Lyness, hidden behind the islands, heard and saw nothing. The nearest ship, from which help might come, was the old seaplane tender *Pegasus*, lying invisible in the gloom nearly two miles away to the west. She remained darkened and silent.

Royal Oak survivors believed that she had seen nothing and heard nothing; indeed, Skipper Gatt said, "They didn't know a rap about what was going on." Witnesses from the *Pegasus* testify otherwise. F. H. Burchett was Corporal of the Gangway when, at 1:04, he looked towards the *Royal Oak* and saw a bright flash from her bow, followed by the sound of her cable running out. The noise was felt down below. Mechanician R. A. Rowley was actually awakened by what he described as "two terrific bangs on the side of the ship." Able Seaman E. Bilton, who was on watch below, recalled, "The whole of the ship vibrated,

* Based on a table compiled by the United States Navy after the war, to prove the ineffectiveness of the Carley raft, which has now been replaced in the Royal Navy by the self-inflating life raft with "Arctic tent"; the raft, in its container, can be carried to the ship's side by two men. If the container goes down with the ship, the raft breaks free and comes to the surface.

the tremor was slight, but I had a feeling something was wrong." Both men went up on deck.

All three saw the series of explosions which followed at about 1:16. "Sheets of flame and debris went up from the *Oak*, followed by more explosions," said Burchett; "four brilliant blue flashes running from fore to aft—in the light of the last flash she seemed to be rolling over to starboard," said Bilton; "sheets of flame and sparks leapt into the air from her fore and after hatches and from her single funnel, accompanied by three explosions," said Rowley.

Then someone began to shout, "Mechanician Rowley! Mechanician Rowley!" Rowley dashed along the upper deck, in pajamas and greatcoat, and was ordered up into the speedboat (saved from the sunken *Courageous*); commanded by Lieutenant Commander Metherall, it was dropped into the water and, with two men in the bow ready to shine flashlights, headed for the scene of the disaster. Meanwhile, the Quartermaster was racing through the ship, piping "Away all boats' crews!" Bilton scrambled into a whaler, the crew of which joined him, half-dressed, within seconds; and they also set off over the dark water, hauling at their oars.

Edwin Wheeler, a Gosport man, deck hand in the Admiralty waterboat *Fountain* lying at that moment tied to Lyness stone jetty, slept on, unaware that hundreds of his fellow townsmen were dead or dying at the other end of the Flow. Police Constable David Allan, on duty in the streets of Kirkwall, thought it would be a night just like any other; he had a friend in the *Royal Oak* but did not suspect that he was then swimming for his life in the black water some three or four miles away. Afterwards, a well-known Orcadian recalled that it must have been that night he had been out walking with his cousin and that they had

commented on the brilliance of the "Merry Dancers"—the
northern lights—and that they had begun to recite from
memory Aytoun's lines,

> *Fearful lights that never beckon*
> *Save when kings and heroes die.*

But this must have been before midnight, because the survivors recall only an ordinary starlit night, with no moon.
Commander Nichols did think he saw northern lights
about the time of the first explosion, but will go only as far
as "a fair aurora." The men in the water could see the
nearest cliffs, half a mile away, because they were silhouetted, but that was all; at first, they could not even see
the *Daisy,* nor could they see other swimmers, unless their
heads were very close.

There were no searchlights sweeping the Flow, no signal
lamps flashing, no destroyers hunting for a submarine, and
no depth charges exploding. There were only bursts of
singing from little groups of men in the water, and screams
and cries from others, with "S O S, S O S, S O S" hooting
from the *Daisy's* whistle. After a little while, two lights
came on.

As the *Daisy* backed away from the sinking battleship,
men in the water were already clinging to the seven auto-
mobile tires tied to her sides as fenders. Hearn was hanging on to one, and four or five other men were holding on
to him; he was in pain from his burns, but did not let go
his hold. One man only was aboard from the battleship,
staggering about dazed. Gatt and his crew began to haul
out of the water the men clinging to the starboard side—
there were at least twenty of them. The *Royal Oak* had already gone from sight, it had taken about seven minutes,
thought Gatt. Then, while his crew threw out pieces of

wood, he lifted a hatch to see what damage the drifter had sustained in sliding off the battleship's blister. It was in fact considerable, but she was not leaking very much, so Gatt assumed she was all right for the moment. But the swimmers in the water were spread out over many hundreds of yards; most of them could not see where the *Daisy* was, or even if she was still afloat; still less could anyone in the *Daisy* see them.

The drifter's funnel was painted white, so Gatt lit a gas lamp at the front of the wheelhouse and another on top, and this, shining on the funnel, was visible at least for several hundred yards. He thought that to show any more light would be imprudent; he did not know what had sunk the *Royal Oak*. Nor did anyone else. Some of the men in the water saw the lights at once, and to the ragged choruses of "Roll Out the Barrel" and "South of the Border" was now added a third melody, "Daisy, Daisy, Give Me Your Answer, Do."

Very close to the *Daisy* were two groups of men, visible from her deck. The mate called out, "Hard a port!" and Gatt, in the wheelhouse, obeyed; then he turned to starboard, to pick up the second group; and after that, seeing no more, lay stopped, waiting for the men somewhere in the outer darkness to swim to him. He knew they were there, he could hear them calling; and he shouted back, "Swim towards us, we'll do our best."

Benton, who was picked up almost immediately, while the *Daisy* was still moving, heard the drifter before he saw her; from the sound of her screw thrashing the water, he thought he was going to be run down, then realized that here was a means of saving himself. He grabbed for one of the rubber tires, missed it, missed the next one, and caught hold of the last, to which other men were already clinging. When they started shouting, a deck hand looked over the side, got another man to help him, and began to haul the swimmers aboard.

He found himself in the boiler room, with about twenty others, all of them merely wet. They all took off their clothes, wrung them out, then put them on again. "Then," said Benton, "the oily ones started coming in, and in very gentlemanly style we made room for them in the warm part; eventually, down came those who'd been burnt. Skin was hanging in shreds down their arms, there was a lost look in their eyes—they were staring, with mouths half open, saying, 'Don't touch me, don't touch me.' The flesh had slipped down their arms like a woman's gauntlet, folded sometimes over the hands—perhaps that happened when men had to grab hold in order to pull them inboard."

One of the first of these lost creatures was Ordnance Artificer Dommett. He had swum away from the ship when she was upside down, with a feeling of irritation all over his body; it was the burned fragments of pajamas rubbing on his seared flesh. He freed himself from these charred remains, saw the light appear on the *Daisy*, and headed towards it, fearful that she would move away. His cries were answered by voices telling him to hold on, there were many more swimmers coming on behind him. "Then," said Dommett, "in that dark night, with only the reflections of the *Daisy's* light on the water as relief, I became conscious of a darker wave rolling up towards me and as it swept over and passed me I knew I was in a sea of oil."

When that wave passed on, the white faces and arms of the unburned swimmers became black, making them virtually invisible in the darkness.

"After what appeared an age I reached the starboard quarter of the drifter and two fellows held a pole over the side for me to climb up. It was only then I realized I was in a bad way. As I held up my hands to grasp the pole, they gasped, 'That poor devil can't climb—look at his hands.' Still, with their efforts I got aboard, naked except for my liberal coating of oil fuel. The lads led me just as I was down below and put me in one of their bunks. I often wonder and hope they were issued with new kit and thanked."

Some of the uninjured survivors now began to help with the hard work of getting slippery, oil-covered swimmers out of the water; others helped them below, first to the boiler room, then the crews' cabin, and finally, to the fish hold, as more and more men had to be crammed into the drifter. Some officer survivors, including Lieutenant Duncan, helped supervise the rescue work, while a lieutenant commander took over at the whistle, continually sending out "S O S," without any apparent effect. Other survivors, including Batterbury, went back into the water time and again to help out men too far gone to help themselves.

Batterbury also had been overtaken by the oil, as he swam away with half a dozen other men in a ragged line from the port side of the *Royal Oak*. He felt as though he were swimming completely in oil, not in water at all, and his movements became sluggish, although he was a strong swimmer. It was too much for the Marine N.C.O., laboring along in his greatcoat. He called, "Cheerio, fellers, I can't hang on"—and was gone.

There was a Carley raft nearby but it was well loaded, so Batterbury made for the cover of a fish hatch, probably thrown out from the *Daisy*, on which a man was lying unconscious. All this took place in a matter of minutes, because the belly of the *Royal Oak* was still visible, with men moving about on it, and almost immediately the *Daisy* came by and Batterbury climbed up a rope into her. After that, the *Daisy* lay stopped, moving only in response to shouts from out of the darkness. The by now oil-blackened faces of the swimmers made a visual search impossible; there was also the danger of ramming the submerged hull of the wreck and further opening the *Daisy's* plates. It was a great strain on Skipper Gatt who, from the wheelhouse, could see very little.

Before the ship had even disappeared Instance, swimming weakly away from the stern, heard a voice calling him from out of the darkness. It was, he thought, his divisional officer, Lieutenant A. H. Terry, clinging to a piece of wood. "Who are you?" called the voice.

He shouted back, "I'm Instance, and I'm burned to beggary."

"Hard luck, old man," came the reply, "but we'll be all right here."

After five or ten minutes of hanging on to the wood, they saw a light, which was the *Daisy,* and the officer suggested swimming to it. Instance willingly agreed, but at once found he could not keep up; after a few strokes he stopped, floundered around, swallowed some water—which turned out to be oil—and could no longer see the officer, who had disappeared ahead in the gloom. But he was not going to drown now, and somehow kept afloat for what may have been half an hour, until he heard another voice calling him in the darkness. Someone said, "Hang on, we're coming," and a small raft appeared, paddled by three men, one of whom was Shipwright Warrant Officer Harding. The raft was probably only half a raft, and the paddle was merely a piece of driftwood.

Someone caught hold of his hands and tried to pull him up onto the raft. Instance screamed in agony. He did not know until that moment just how badly he had been burned. Somone else called, "Pull him up by his hair." But he had no hair. Eventually they got a grip under his arm pits and hauled him in that way. Instance sat there, so grateful for his rescue that he tried to help paddle by using his hands; then he passed out.

Around the sunken bow, several Carley rafts were bobbing about in the water; one of them complete and undamaged. Leading Telegraphist Jones, after skidding down the side, surfaced to find this one only a few feet away from him, so some devoted group must have managed to get it away before the battleship turned over. A moment or so later Commander Nichols, who had only abandoned ship when she gave her final lurch, joined him on the raft. Shortly afterwards, Chief Stoker Terry arrived and soon the raft was so heavily loaded with men that it sank beneath them; Jones, who is a tall man, found himself up to his chest in water, but still standing on the raft. Some of the men then got off, and as it rose to the surface again, hung on to the sides.

Struggling in the water nearby, hampered by watch coat and sea boots, was Leading Signalman Fossey. From another buckled raft the two boys, Trewinnard and Upham, heard him splashing and shouting in a dazed fashion, "Is there any boats?" They managed to pull him to their raft, which was of use only to cling to, then saw the other complete raft a short distance away. A man shouted to them that it was too full, but as Fossey was injured, they ignored that and Jones put out a hand and hauled Fossey to safety. Chief Stoker Lawrence, who had gone in at the same time and place as Commander Nichols, also owed his life to a friend. Unable to swim, because he had injured his right arm in going over, he remembers hooking his left arm round a plank. Chief Mechanician Kim also had hold of the plank, and, unknown to Lawrence, held on to him for forty-five minutes until they were found by the *Daisy*.

Captain Benn must have found the buckled raft, or an-

other like it, because he was reported to have said afterwards that he had thought he was doing well until he saw
Commander Nichols go past him on his "Rolls Royce." In
point of fact the Carley raft is not adapted to progression
and this one was going round in circles. It was certainly
doing so when, after what seemed to him a long time,
Blundell reached it. He was on his way to the shore and
nearly done; he had taken off his wrist watch, because he
thought the tiny weight might make just that bit of difference, but he hung on to his belt with the £13 1s. od. in it.
A strong swimmer, he had not reckoned on the oil, which
seemed a foot thick at least. At the raft, they made room
for him to hang on to the side, one injured man growl-
ing, "Mind my bloody arm."

To help propel the raft, he began kicking out with his
legs. There were no paddles, and people on the raft were
using their hands. When they saw the lights of the *Daisy*
come on, there were shouts of, "Make for that light." Other
men, however, thought the shore was nearer, and paddled
in that direction. The raft lurched along in circles; but the
effort kept them warm and some began singing. Fossey, lying on it, with a finger almost torn off and one leg completely numb, dimly remembers "South of the Border" and
the inevitable "Roll Out the Barrel."

It was deathly quiet all around them now, partly because they were moving away towards the cliffs and partly
because the shouting and screaming in the water had
ceased. There was an ominous reason for that.

When Sims had swarmed down into the picket boat, she
had cast off but, having no steam up, had remained rocking in the water beside the heeling battleship until Wilson
and one or two others had got men to lie down by the gunwales and paddle with their hands. Then, already overloaded, she proved a magnet for every man swimming near

her; Boxall reached her before the *Royal Oak* sank, and got
on deck, which was packed with men, sitting and standing.
The forepeak, engine room, and after cabin were crammed
with men and her sides were nearly awash. Kerr, badly
burned, swam to her but found the sides jammed with
men hanging on and threshing the water; he got a grip,
but the men on either side of him seemed in a very bad
way, so he backstroked clear to give them more room. She
was swaying dangerously, but someone in her started up
with "South of the Border, Down Mexico Way" and those
in the water joined in.

Suddenly the singing stopped, as another rush of swimmers came away from the battleship and made for the
picket boat, which was heeling over to starboard. Wilson
heard someone shout, "Trim the dish," in an attempt to
right her, and saw men obediently go over to the port side.
She heeled immediately to port and half the men on deck,
including Wilson and Sims, were thrown over into the water. Some of them, in falling or diving off, struck Kerr, who
hurriedly backed away. Once off, most of them swam back
to get on again, but Sims had had enough and he swam
away, seeing as he did so the *Royal Oak* rolling over and
the flash of a last explosion somewhere near the quarter-
deck. Boxall, who was still hanging on by the funnel of the
picket boat, estimated that less than six minutes had
elapsed since the second explosion and thought, quite
correctly, that she sank partly on her starboard side. Apart
from the *Daisy*, and a few battered rafts and bits of wood,
the picket boat was the only hope for the badly wounded
men among the swimmers.

Kerr heard someone calling for help but, himself terribly
burned, could do no more than urge the man on. "Come
on," he shouted," only a few more yards."

"I can't do it, I can't do it," cried the man but, with Kerr shouting encouragement, by a supreme effort he eventually made the side of the picket boat.

Saltmarsh was out in the darkness, blinded by oil fuel and sick from having swallowed some of it; he had been sitting on the bottom of the ship when someone behind said, "Get into the water, you silly bastard!" and gave him a push. "I landed," said Saltmarsh, "in a whacking great pool of sludge, and got a bellyful of it." Struggling blindly, he heard a voice calling, "Make for the pinnace," then felt himself dragged up by the arms. Still unable to see a thing, he found himself sitting on what felt like cushions, presumably in the stern sheets of the picket boat, and heard men shouting, "We're overloaded, we've got too many as it is."

Wilson had fallen overboard at the first lurch, at last losing the flashlight to which he had so tenaciously clung, but had climbed back on again, only to hear once more a shout of "Trim the dish!" As men tried to move over to the starboard side, the port side came level, then rose higher—and the picket boat turned over.

Saltmarsh, still completely blind, found himself threshing about in the water, worried by his oil-filled jersey, which felt like an "armor-plated jacket." He struggled out of it, at once felt the intense cold—and felt something bump against him. It seemed to be a horsehair cushion from the picket boat. He grabbed at it and lost consciousness.

Wilson came to the surface amid a tremendous free-for-all of howling, screaming men. Arms grabbed hold of him and he found himself well down under the water, gripped by two men. He did not remember much of the struggle except that he managed to shove them off him and that when he broke surface all his clothes had gone—all he was wearing was a waistbelt and one leg of his pajama trousers.

He struck away at once from the circle of shouting, threshing, drowning swimmers.

On the edge of the arc it was quieter, there were only a few swimmers. He saw some of them throw up their hands and drown. One man said something like, "Sorry, mate, sorry," before he disappeared. Wilson knew he must not get too far away, or he would never be found. He began to feel the cold. "It got past my flesh," he said, "until I could feel my own skeleton. I was aware of every bone in my body."

Boxall jumped clear as the picket boat went over, but, seeing that she was still afloat, with an air lock in her compartments, he swam back and got onto the keel. There must have been at that moment some thirty or forty men trapped inside, upside down. Many more swimmers came to join him, clambering up out of the water at the stern. So many climbed up that, within a minute or so, she sank stern first and disappeared forever. Boxall went back into the water and swam around for a while, until he found a boat's chock to hold on to.

Somewhere about this time Mrs. Evelyn Booth, seven hundred miles to the south, wakened from sleep by a disturbing dream, lay listening to the wind howling round the house in Southsea. What was the dream? She could not remember, but it had been about her husband and he was somehow safe from something. There had been a loud noise, too. But perhaps that had really been the blackout curtain, blown down by the wind. Somehow comforted, she turned over and went to sleep again.

George Booth, whose last memory had been of lying across a ladder inside the *Royal Oak*, and of tremendous waves of noise in his ears, recovered consciousness to find himself in the water, with what seemed to be half a gale blowing; it was very dark and cold, and he was stark naked, clutching a cigarette lighter in his hand. Dimly, he remembered that it was a present from his wife, arrived in the mail the day before. He swam slowly, hardly conscious of what he was doing. After a little while, he saw another man in the water; curiously, the man was swimming with only one arm. As Booth went towards him, he recognized a friend—and saw, too, at the man's shoulder, a mess of flesh and bone where the left arm had been. Before Booth could do or say anything, the dying Sergeant cried out, "Cheerio, chaps," threw up his one arm, and sank.

McLaverty was trying to save a Maltese, who was shouting and crying out; he grabbed him by the shirt, saying, "What's up, Joe?" But the Maltese was frantic, and kept turning over and over in the water, threshing wildly, until his shirt—which McLaverty still had hold of—was twisted like a rope. The Mediterranean was no sort of training for a swim in Scapa Flow in winter. McLaverty got his legs round the Maltese, trying to keep his head above the water that way, and calling out, "Why don't you speak to me, Josie?" But the man gave no reply and in a little while was as stiff as a poker, with McLaverty's hand frozen to his shirt.

Finley, his burns caked now in oil, was too weak to swim far. Most of the time he just trod water and tried to keep up; above all, he wanted to keep the oil out of his mouth. At first there were terrible cries all around him, then they died away to an ominous silence. Two men appeared, splashing towards him. They asked if he could help them, but Finley managed to reply that he could hardly help himself. They made no attempt to grab hold of him, but carried on hopelessly, obviously not likely to last much longer.

Finley felt his strength ebbing, and was half resigned to going under, when he seemed to see green fields and felt, almost audibly, something saying, "It's not your turn—keep going." It was a sort of conscious hallucination, for he was seeing and hearing it in his mind—there was a face in it somewhere, too—and he was aware also, all the time, of his family and the need to keep alive for them. Just after that had put heart into him, a mast or spar came by, with a man sitting on the middle of it and another man on one end. This was real enough, and Finley caught hold of the free end, but he never did find out who the other two men were.

Almost immediately he saw a light—it was the *Daisy*, lying stopped—and they began to work their way towards it. When only a few yards away, the mast began to roll; the man at the far end vanished and did not reappear. Then Finley felt arms round him, lifting him, and solid deck under his feet; someone was saying, "The chap's pretty bad." He was put into the Skipper's bunk and Gatt himself, with all his other worries, turned the blankets so that the woolen side would not stick to his flesh. Finley knew only that he was in the Skipper's bunk, but Gatt remembered him, because the burned flesh was hanging in strips down his arms. Finley recalled asking for a drink of water, and of sitting up and looking at Leading Supply Assistant Sims. Sims had a life belt on, and Finley shouted, "Where'd you get that from?"

"I remember nothing else," he said, "except a lieutenant having a terrible attack of hysterics, laughing and that; and people trying to calm him down. There was no pain yet—I just felt horrible. The oil was keeping my burns covered and I couldn't see what had happened to me."

Booth, floating in the water, suddenly felt a sharp pain under his arm pit, and found the *Daisy* above him and a man with a boat hook hauling him to the side. Very far gone indeed, he was laid down on something cold and

soft. When he revived enough to look round, he saw that
it was a pile of oil-soaked corpses. He noticed an arm moving feebly, and dragged the man clear—the face looked as
if soot had been forced into it, so terrible were the burns.
That feeble movement was almost the last; the man died
within a few minutes.

McLaverty also was too far gone to see the *Daisy*, he
only heard the thud-thud of an engine and a shout, "Get a-
hold of this line." He never could have grasped it but, being wet, it wrapped itself round his right arm. "They pulled
me up like a shark, ripping me on the barnacles; I felt that,
with salt water in the cuts." At that moment, the body of
the Maltese, long since frozen stiff, fell away from Mc-
Laverty's grasp as the man's shirt tore.

The cold was so intense that even the strong swimmers
were glad to get hold of any sort of support in the water;
most of those who were afloat for any length of time, and
survived, had found something to keep them up while they
swam. Cadet Owen and a young Marine clung to the same
piece of wood, and just waited to be found. Barry Hawes
also had a bit of wood, but when he saw that another man
a few yards away had a life belt, he asked if he could
share it. Then, together, each with one arm locked in the
life belt, they swam for the drifter. Sergeant Parham,
not a good swimmer, thought he was in luck when a wave
bounced something off his head and he found that it was a
life belt. Even so, the real seriousness of his position, prior
to that, never really struck home. When picked up, he
threw back the life belt for someone else. Most of the men,
now, had to be hauled out; if a line was thrown and they
grabbed it, they usually fell back at the last moment. Paymaster Commander Cundall, burned but still wearing his
cap, twice saw the *Daisy* turn away from him at the last
moment to rescue someone else; Flag-Lieutenant Affleck-

Graves pulled him aboard. Able Seaman Farley had been clinging to a bit of wood for two and a half hours when he was found; too far gone to swim, he could still shout. "Keep shouting," yelled a voice out of the darkness, "we'll find out where you are, then." A line was thrown to him, but he was too weak even to grasp it, so a *Royal Oak* man, it may have been Batterbury, jumped again into the icy water with a line and tied it round Farley, who, so he said, was just about ready to hand in his insurance policy. As he was hauled up, he was recognized, and there was a delighted shout of "Oh, it's you, you fat so-and-so!"

There was at least one boat floating waterlogged; this was the gig, with its cover still in place. A number of survivors describe seeing it, and say they were the only person there, which is probable, because no one stayed long on it, it was warmer in the icy water. Some said it was floating right way up, and others upside down; and that, too, was quite possible, for it turned over on the slightest provocation. Engineer Commander Renshaw reached it early when the propellers of the capsized battleship were still faintly visible against the night sky. He estimated he was there forty-five minutes, sometimes on the canopy and sometimes on the keel. Stanley Rowlands passed it, and thought he saw a number of men trying to get on. Not a strong swimmer, and now with his foot broken, he had tried for five minutes to keep a young Marine afloat. The man made no move to help himself and Rowlands thought he was probably dead, and left him. After seeing the boat he remembered nothing more until, several hours later, he found himself in the *Daisy*.

After a long time, Renshaw saw the *Daisy* and remembered that he still had his flashlight in his pocket. He pulled it out and, to his surprise, it worked, so he flashed it on and off in the direction of the drifter. Eventually she steamed towards him and, when she was a hundred yards away, he slipped into the water and swam towards her. It was Renshaw who gave Skipper Gatt the fright of his life.

"When we had about 250 survivors on board," wrote Gatt a few months later, "I thought the game was up; for, when I looked out on our port side, there was a light coming through the water, and I thought it was a torpedo. But it turned out to be a sailor with a lighted torch in his mouth, so you may know the relief that came to me when I saw what it was." The light must have seemed curious, for the flashlight was covered in oil.

The gig was now abandoned, and Boxall was probably the next to reach it. He had first tried the picket boat, then a piece of wood; the gig proved equally unsatisfactory. "I was sitting on the bows," said Boxall, "only my stern sheets in the water; but I got so cold there, in the wind, that I got back into the water again. Around me was only black darkness; I heard plenty of shouting, but couldn't see any lights." He never saw the *Daisy* at all, until he was pulled on board and put in the wheelhouse. Only one other man went into the wheelhouse, because Skipper Gatt needed room to con the drifter in the darkness.

Wilson was next to find the gig; he saw it first as a dark shadow in the water, riding submerged and waterlogged. He climbed on, got his chest out of the water, then, like Boxall, decided it was warmer in the icy sea, and simply hung on to its side. He did see the lights of the *Daisy* but, as she was approaching him, she went off on another tack. When she eventually came back, he heard a shout of, "There he is." Men leaned over him and started to hoist him in over the bow, but his numbed hands could no longer grip, and he fell back into the water, to a disgusted shout of, "Don't muck around in the aquatic!" He had been in the water one and a half hours.

The strain on Gatt was immense. With every boat gone
and only one intact Carley raft afloat, the whole burden of
saving life fell on him. As hour succeeded hour, peering
out into the darkness to avoid ramming the wreck, ma-
neuvering a few yards towards faint voices coming from
here, there and everywhere, and going below to see the
wounded attended to, he became desperately tired. There
was still no sign of life in the Flow, it was all entirely up to
him. In all, he saved 386 men—almost all the survivors
owed their lives to him and his crew.

At least fifty men tried to swim to the shore, half a mile
away, but less than twenty reached it. Although it was a
calm night, there was a bad "lop" on the water; the northeast wind, coming from over the cliffs, blew the tops of the
waves into the swimmers' faces when they tried to go in
that direction. Petty Officer Kerr, after leaving the picket
boat, found himself alone, "it seemed on a wide, wide sea,"
but got a mouthful of water when he struck out for the
shore. So he turned round and breast stroked in the opposite direction, which was much easier. If he had headed a
little further to the left he would have gone out into the
middle of Scapa Flow and drowned somewhere in the
gloom. Eventually he saw two white lights, which did not
move; as he went slowly towards them two men paddled
past him on a piece of wreckage—probably part of a Carley
float—and disappeared into the darkness. At length, laboring badly, he saw that the lights were actually the anchor
lights of a fairly large ship. It was the *Pegasus*. With the
skin burned off his head, neck and hands, he had swum
two miles in icy water, and had taken at least two hours
and forty-five minutes to do it.

By 3:55, two and a half hours after the sinking, there was
silence around the *Daisy;* there were no more voices calling from the water. The drifter was dangerously full of

men and many of them needed medical attention urgently. Skipper Gatt decided to discontinue the search and take the survivors to the *Pegasus*.

By now, some of the boats from the *Pegasus* had reached the scene and had begun to search with flashlights for survivors. At about 4:10 A.M., the *Daisy II* went alongside the seaplane carrier, to discharge her cargo of shocked and burned men. "There were no lights from the *Pegasus*," said Gatt, "as they didn't know what had happened until we went alongside the gangway." Surgeon Commander St. George B. Delisle Gray, of the hospital ship *Aba*, testifies that it was at about four A.M. that they received a signal "*Royal Oak* sunk," and immediately began to make preparations to receive casualties.

It was probably about this time that the *Pegasus* briefly switched on her signal projector; it blazed in short flashes only, as it was not designed for continuous burning. The men in the intact Carley raft saw it, but it did not illuminate them. Bendell, still swimming, saw it, too; it went backwards and forwards across the water, but did not reach him. It did, however, enable him to see for the first time that there was another man near him in the water; his head was black with fuel oil and, as Bendell made towards him, he went under suddenly and did not reappear. The light was, in fact, being directed on the cliff top, in case any survivors had managed to climb up there. It momentarily lit up a strange vessel heading for Holm Sound, which Bilton thought afterwards might have been a U-boat but was probably one of the drifters which were now coming out from Scapa Pier to search the shore for exhausted swimmers.

The oared boats from the *Pegasus* had had a long pull to the scene. "We raced in the direction of where the *Royal Oak* should be," recalled Bilton. "Those two miles seemed to be an eternity and in the pitch darkness it wasn't an easy task looking for survivors, we had to keep stopping, listening and searching the black waters. We found one group of men hanging on to some kind of float, one was an officer, a commander, I was told; another rating was fully clothed, oilskin, sea boots and all. One most vivid in my mind was, we had stopped to listen, then I saw an arm raise slowly in the water about ten feet away. I lifted my oar and dropped it in front of him, narrowly missing his head by inches. He grabbed it and was saved."

The latter may have been Bendell, who was one of the last, if not the last to be rescued—at about six A.M., he was told. A strong swimmer, now a member of Portsmouth Lifeguards, he had made for the shore, then oil had clogged his movements. It was a ghastly feeling, as if someone was trying to drag him back; he was more frightened then than in the sunken compartment. So he gave up the attempt and merely tried to keep in the patches of clear water. He shouted, but only became hoarse, and it seemed to do no good. He was very cold and barely conscious. He remembers a boat coming along, and someone yelling at him to grab an oar, which he did. After that, he remembered nothing until he was aboard the *Pegasus*.

A batch of men had already been taken off from the intact Carley raft, but there was not enough room for all of them and those who had to wait—it seemed an age—included Commander Nichols and the injured Fossey, wearing his greatcoat and seaboots. Blundell had already become impatient, and swum to a boat which he had seen in the distance. It was this remnant of the survivors on the Carley which were picked up by Bilton's whaler. Bilton remembers the Commander rambling, "Pull for the shore, lads, pull for the shore." Fossey's recollection is of being covered with a blanket and of another survivor trying to pull it off him—and a voice saying, "You touch him again, and we'll throw you over the side."

Kerr, laboring towards the anchor lights of the *Pegasus*, saw that there was a drifter alongside the gangway, the *Daisy* disembarking survivors. Batterbury, from the landing stage, was helping to pull an injured paymaster out of the water, he thought it might have been Lieutenant Commander Maclean. At the same time, other men were helping a terribly burned man onto the landing stage; from the description it was Instance. "It sticks in my mind," said Batterbury, "flesh was running like water from his hands and face, more from the hands than the face. He was holding them in front of him, like downward-pointing claws, and the flesh was dripping off them. I remember being genuinely surprised at what burning could do: I had no idea anything like this happened. I also remember feeling astonished because he was not in pain—at any rate, not to the extent of the damage done to him. He didn't howl, but just acted as you would if you'd jammed your finger in something. I seem to remember they covered him with a blanket."

Instance, who had arrived on the buckled Carley raft, perhaps the one Kerr had seen go past him, was not in fact conscious at that moment; or at any rate, has no memory of it. But he did recall what happened less than a minute later, as he was being taken to the gangway. He heard a seaman say, "He's got a belt round his waist." Another seaman answered, "Sling it away, then we'll get a blanket over him."

Instance sat up with a jerk. "Not on your nelly," he shouted, "my money's in that!"

But Kerr screamed out in pain when two men knelt down from the landing stage and grabbed him by the hands. He heard one of them call, "Throw down a line, he's a big chap." They put the line round him and hoisted his two-hundred-ten-pound weight on to the *Daisy*. "Then it started," said Kerr, "I began to tremble and shiver with cold and shock."

Instance and Kerr, like all the men who had been burned, were not in pain until someone touched them; they merely felt weak and ill, and shivered uncontrollably. The agony was reserved for later.

10

"Regret *Royal Oak* Has Sunk"

In accordance with instructions for patrol duties, Police Constable David H. Allan called in at Kirkwall Police Station during the early hours of the morning, while these scenes were taking place a few miles away; but he cannot now remember exactly the time. While there, a telephone call came through which resulted in his being told to go out with another constable, wake a local bus hirer, and get a bus sent to Scapa Pier as quickly as possible. As they were hurrying along they met a civilian, who told them that the *Royal Oak* had been sunk.

While he was doing this, Edwin Wheeler, sleeping in the water boat *Fountain* which was tied up to Lyness stone jetty, was awakened by a lieutenant commander or commander who was asking for the Master of the vessel. Very shortly afterwards the *Fountain* raised steam and began to move up through the destroyer anchorage towards Rysa Sound and Hoy Sound, which held at this moment a number of coasters being used as store ships. They stopped at each one and passed the order, "Raise steam and prepare to leave Scapa at one hour's notice." They were now told

120

by the Master that the *Royal Oak* had sunk at her anchorage.

The reason for all this minor activity was that three survivors, having swum half a mile to the shore, had still sufficient strength left to walk the two miles to Scapa and wake the Pier Master. He telephoned the *Iron Duke,* ten miles away at Lyness, and she made to *Pegasus,* "What has happened?" *Pegasus* promptly sent back, "Regret *Royal Oak* has sunk."

The fishing drifters at Scapa Pier were getting up steam; some of them concentrated their search close inshore along the rocky cliffs opposite the sunken battleship and were later joined by one of the whalers from the *Pegasus.* They cruised slowly along, calling out in the night to anyone who might be lying on the rocks. Here and there came back an answer.

When Stoker Cleverley, still unaware of his burns, went off from the starboard side of the quarter-deck, he found himself among a group of perhaps fifty men. Among them was a lieutenant who called out to them, "No use waiting for boats—swim to the shore." And off they went. Among them were Boy A. W. Scovell and Ordinary Seaman R. ("Pincher") Martin, both of whom are now lieutenants. Scovell was one of the strong swimmers; perfectly at home in the water, he spent most of his holidays swimming and had competed for his school. Apart from the cold and the oil, it was an easy twenty-minute swim, the "lop" which bothered the moderate swimmers and the badly injured was of no real account to anyone used to swimming head down, mouth under water most of the time. He plugged on steadily until he saw ahead of him the fluorescence where the waves were breaking on the rocks. After he had climbed out of the water, it was very cold; he just huddled there on his own, trying to keep warm.

Cleverley had a rough idea of the direction to take, and after a while could make out the dim loom of the cliffs; behind him in the Flow it was quite dark, with no land to be seen. He remembers nothing more until he was climbing up the rocks; after getting perhaps ten feet out of the water he collapsed and lost consciousness, he had no idea why.

Lieutenant Keen had never before swum more than a hundred yards. But soon after skidding down the quarterdeck and being pitched into the sea, he found a bit of wood and locked his arms round it while he kicked out with his feet. His first instinct, thinking of the *Vanguard*, was to get away; next, he was obsessed with a fear that he might swim right out of the Flow, through Hoxa Sound, so he turned left for the shore. He took a long time to reach it and, if he had not found the wood, certainly would never have done so. "I was getting rather numb," is how he described it, "as though I was slowly going to sleep, there was no discomfort or anything. I was mentally and physically tired, not really thinking of anything, not cold, not frightened, not uncomfortable, just doing a sort of breast stoke with the wood under my arms."

Even so, there were reserves of strength. "I suddenly woke up in a very vigorous way, because I heard waves breaking. It was pretty calm, so I knew I must be near to shore, and I suddenly swam like mad. I must have dashed into the rocks, because I remember my head banging against them. I came to, with a few cuts on face and head, jolly pleased at having something solid to hold on to."

For a while Keen lay there, half in and half out of the water, then he started to climb—the rocks were sharp and hard to his bare feet—tripped, and fell over a boy seaman. Both of them were totally exhausted and covered in oil. After a rest, they began to climb the cliff, hoping to make their way inland and find a farm; but they were as weak as kittens and, in the dark, the attempt appeared dangerous. Someone else, to their left, was also scrambling up, to judge by the noises; the sounds ended abruptly in a cry and a thump.

That decided them to wait for daylight, so they huddled together for warmth. Then they saw, only a few feet away, two white circles moving closer towards them. It was a second or so before Keen realized that it was the whites of a man's eyes. They asked the apparition who it was, and it said that it was Leading Telegraphist so-and-so. He was completely black with oil and even at a distance of two feet only his eyes could be seen. They all lay down, to get as much out of the wind as possible, and drifted off into unconsciousness.

Some time between four and five o'clock Cleverley was awakened by shouting. A whaler was coming along by the rocks, with men calling out, "Anyone there?" He shouted back, and was taken off. A few minutes later they found Scovell who, because they could not risk the boat by coming close inshore at that point, had to swim out to them. They were all feeling rather lightheaded now that they were safe. When Scovell gave his name, "Pincher" Martin, who had also reached the land and was already in the boat, bellowed out, "You can throw that back!"

Somewhere nearby they could hear splashing—it was probably another man who had got ashore previously, Scovell had heard him shouting. Now, they thought, he must be trying to swim out to the whaler. They looked, but never found him. There were reports afterwards of a number of sailors found dead on the shore, their arms outstretched as if to grasp the rocks. Constable Allan was in fact called down a few days afterwards to one such body, naked and covered in fuel oil. "My thoughts were," he said, "that this poor fellow probably saved himself from the sea that tragic morning, but had dropped exhausted on reaching the shore, and died of exposure."

The most curious thing about it all, thought Cleverley later, was that, after first being burned, then thrown into the icy sea, and finally exposed naked for hours to a bitter wind, he himself suffered not even so much as a cold, let alone pneumonia; nor did anyone else that he heard of.

Eventually the whaler had some seven or eight men on board, and transferred them to a fishing drifter which had come out from Scapa to help. When trying to get warm on the engine room gratings, Cleverley discovered for the first time that he had been burned—he was a hospital case for more than three weeks afterwards—and that he was still holding in his hand the sodden box of matches which he had grabbed from above his hammock just before the third explosion.

At Scapa Pier a crowd was waiting. Constable Allan was now there with the civilian bus and Cleverley was carried to it; he was rather resentful, he felt quite all right. They were wrapped in white blankets, and he thought what a shame it was to ruin them. Fifteen men in all were landed at Scapa Pier and taken to the Kirkwall Hotel, which had been requisitioned by the Navy. Cleverley found himself perched on a chair by the fire, with his legs up, opposite Chief Stoker C. Hine. Anything they liked to drink they could have. "Lofty and I sat there drinking whisky as if it was water, and talking. I had no eyebrows, my hair was all gone on one side, my right ear was burnt, also my feet and lower legs." People crowded round, bombarding them with questions; their names were taken and, within a few hours, these fifteen became the first list of survivors to be issued by the Admiralty.

Constable Allan helped to get some of them out to the Naval airdrome at Hatston, where Cleverley was put in what he thought was the sub-lieutenants' dormitory. "I didn't have much time for officers," he said, "but those Fleet Air Arm people were very good; they got us a radio, and one of them gave me his pajama jacket, which was all I had in the way of clothes."

Meanwhile, Keen and the two others with him had missed their chance of figuring in the first list. He woke up, becoming conscious of a light, and crawled to the edge of the rocks. A fishing drifter was close inshore, shining an Aldis lamp up and down the cliffs; closer inshore still was the drifter's dingy. Keen crawled back to wake the other two. "I was beastly to them," he said, "I kept hitting and thumping them, but they didn't stir." He turned to call out to the two men in the dingy and a braw Scots voice replied, "Aw reet, we're here."

Then he was in the stokehold of the drifter. "The three of us were sitting there like three old black crows by the furnace; I, very well-dressed in my pajamas, the boy in a vest and one sock, the leading tel. in one sock. A man who was down there, doing the coaling and answering the telegraph, handed us a huge mug of tea—with something in it. I told him about the chap I'd heard falling down the cliff, and he shouted the information up the voice-pipe to the Skipper." A search revealed nothing and the drifter took them, not to Scapa Pier, but out to the *Pegasus*.

The Fleet water carrier *Fountain* took some three hours to complete her task of alerting the store ships and colliers by word of mouth. For the first part of the trip the *Royal Oak*'s anchorage, ten miles to the northeast, was hidden from her view by the island of Fara, but, as she steamed into Gutter Sound, Edwin Wheeler could look right across. They had all expected to see some form of activity, but there was nothing, neither searchlights nor the lights of ships were visible; it was all absolutely dark and quiet.

In fact there were a few drifters and boats cruising over the spot, with dimmed riding lights, searching for survivors with the aid of nothing larger than a flashlight. The *Pegasus,* after briefly switching on a signal lamp, had thought better of it and blacked out again. At about this time Midshipman Pirie was listening to what he called a "slight altercation" between a senior officer from the *Royal Oak* and a senior officer of the *Pegasus.* The *Royal Oak* officer was demanding to know why the *Pegasus* had not switched on a searchlight, and the other was replying, equally forcibly, that he did not wish to be torpedoed as well.

On the other hand, the two destroyers at Lyness remained where they were and no search for a submarine was made until daylight, and this may have been partly because there were other, more plausible, reasons for the disaster being canvassed at that moment. Engineer Commander Renshaw, after a hot bath, went into the wardroom in borrowed clothing and met there Captain Benn and Commander Nichols. Although his first assumption had been that it was a torpedo, the discussion unearthed other possibilities. The *Royal Oak* was the fifth British warship to blow up at anchor—they all remembered the other four cases during the first world war, one of them actually in Scapa. Those never had been explained, although certain alterations to magazines had afterwards been put in hand, In particular, they remembered H.M.S. *Natal,* which had blown up at Invergordon immediately after a children's party had been held on board, during which, quite naturally, a number of nonservice personnel had been in the ship. They were all very much aware of the similarity between that and the storing of the *Royal Oak* a few hours previously. Wherever stores had been put, there had been an explosion; and there was, too, that disquieting gap of twelve minutes between the first explosion and the second, which did not fit at all with the short gaps of a torpedo salvo but *did* fit the irregular unpredictable workings of acid in the fuses of time bombs.

Another conjecture was that an aircraft had laid a string of mines in the anchorage and that the ship had swung at her anchor over them; the tide had in fact been on the turn at about that time. No certain conclusion could be reached, but the general impression was that the *Royal Oak* had been sunk by, as the Flag-Lieutenant expressed it, "an unknown agency." There was a good deal of gloom; if Hitler could do this to them, what would happen to the rest of the Fleet?

The *Pegasus* was the former *Ark Royal*, 6,900 tons, purchased as a seaplane tender in 1914, and now used for transporting aircraft. She was quite the most distinctive ship in the Navy—once seen, never forgotten—with her single spindly funnel and mast apparently in the wrong place. She was not equipped, as a depot ship would have been, to deal with a sudden influx of four hundred sodden, oil-soaked, shocked and wounded men; but she coped magnificently. Her crew gave up their hammocks, their clothes and their kit to the survivors; they turned on hot baths, made tea and cocoa, and poured out rum. They sorted out the unhurt from the wounded, and the badly wounded from the men able to walk, they took names and addresses for notifying next of kin, they asked the hospital ship *Aba* to send her drifter to take off the urgent cases, and they notified Kirkwall that additional medical supplies would be needed.

By six A.M. all the survivors were out of the *Daisy* and being dealt with in the *Pegasus*. Captain Benn then asked Skipper Gatt to go back to the scene of the sinking for a further search, but as fishing drifters from Scapa were now moving about over the spot Gatt thought it was unnecessary; he also thought he had done enough for one night (the Admiralty agreed, they gave him the Distinguished Service Cross). Shortly after, a former fishing drifter, fitted out as a tender to the hospital ship, arrived alongside and began to embark the badly injured. She was so new that the bunks had no mattresses or pillows.

Surgeon Commander G. L. Ritchie now began to get the worst cases into her. Himself a survivor, he had taken a leading part in looking after the wounded. "How that man worked!" said Kerr, who, wrapped in blankets and hot-water bottles and filled with brandy, was still trembling uncontrollably. He was helped down the gangway, gave his name, rating and number to a Marine corporal standing there, and was put into a small cabin with five other men, including Supply Petty Officer Finley, Able Seaman Handforth and Ordinary Seaman Hearn. Then Sick Berth Attendant Bendell was brought in. He had been in the water much longer than most and was suffering from the shock of being trapped inside the ship when she went down; he had hurt his feet and hands badly and was afraid of losing a finger. He was muttering all the time, "Don't take it off, don't take it off!" Dommett, unable to walk, was slung into what had been the fish hold, now equipped with bunks, and squirmed around trying to make a pillow for himself. Instance was just beginning to revive and to feel the pain of his burns—an agony which was to last for many weeks. The men in the cabin were trying rather comically to help each other with drinks and cigarettes, fumbling because their hands were raw. At about 8:15 the drifter got under way for Lyness, where the hospital ship was lying.

Meanwhile, those who could walk had been sent down to the engine and boiler rooms to warm up. Chief Stoker Lawrence, injured, was half carried in by two seamen but, as soon as he saw a boiler, he flung them off and curled

himself round it. He was badgered to drink cocoa, but refused; accepted a cup of coffee and was immediately sick.
After that he felt better. McLaverty was given rum—and
then struck violently in the stomach. He, too, was sick; and
felt better. Batterbury was handed a glass, drank it—and
found it was salt water. That, too, had the desired effect.
Farley was given hot water—and vomited. What came up
was, he said, "just like ink." It was, of course, fuel oil. "They
knew what they were doing, all right," said Batterbury,
wryly. Lieutenant Keen finished the best part of a bottle of
whisky within an hour—it had absolutely no effect, presumably because of his oil-lined stomach; then, trailing
"blood and cinders" from the cuts on his feet, went to look
for survivors from the Royal Marine detachment. There
were pitifully few.

Saltmarsh found himself looking up at some sort of light,
rather like the sun seen through closed eyelids; as his last
recollection was of holding onto a cushion in the night near
the capsized picket boat, he was puzzled. He was still in
the water, but now it was hot. He was in fact being bathed.
Some time later, it may have been days later, he was in a
cabin with a man bending over him saying, "Who are you,
son?" All he could reply was, "I'm a Marine, I'm a Marine."

The idea of the hot baths was to restore lost heat to the
body as well as to remove the fuel oil, but some time during the night the hot water gave out. Blundell, who had to
be carried to the bathroom, was simply wiped down. His
clothes were thrown on to a rapidly growing pile of filthy,
oil-stained garments. Then he was put straight into somebody else's hammock and went off to sleep.

One man, Farley says he was a Scotsman, actually
wasted hot water; naked, he was standing under a tap
washing a bundle of pound notes. When Lawrence came
to, the first man he saw was the Schoolmaster—"a tall,

portly person, he was striding gravely about the boiler room, as naked as the day he was born, except for his shoes." Within half an hour Blundell woke up again, vaguely uneasy; then he remembered that his money belt —with the £13 1s. od. in it—had been thrown onto the heap of filthy clothing. The heap was much larger when he got back to it, but he tore into the pile and found the belt. Much satisfied, he marched back to his hammock.

11

"Believed by U-Boat Action"

After breakfast—and a "Red" air raid warning, which was probably a reconnaissance aircraft—the *Pegasus* got under way for Lyness, where she transferred the survivors to the S.S. *Voltaire*, a former Lamport & Holt liner. They were now among the islands, with the naval base in full view; nearby were the *Aba*, the *Iron Duke*, two destroyers, a collier, and a number of store ships and auxiliaries. As Farley shuffled over the brow into the *Voltaire*, holding up with one hand a pair of trousers much too small for him, he said "Good morning" to a padre standing there to welcome them, and was told that he was the happiest survivor the padre had seen that day—a sight for sore eyes. Then he was given "a good hot breakfast, with lashings of rum," and went off in search of a bathroom. The oil, he said, was oozing out of him for two weeks afterwards.

Intent on a second breakfast, Lieutenant Keen came into the mess, which was of course new to him, and saw a number of strange faces, the *Voltaire's* officers. A grumpy old Commander asked him who he was, so Keen replied that he was ex-*Royal Oak*. "Sabotage!" grunted the Commander. "I thought so! Always said it would happen." No one said a word; that was what they all feared it was.

During the rest of the morning and afternoon there was steady methodical activity in the Flow; minesweepers were at work, searching for a possible submarine or for any torpedoes which had missed their target, and picket boats armed with a single depth charge balanced on the stern were cruising about. Nothing was found, except the Barrel of Butter buoy, several times reported as a conning tower. And that was odd.

Assuming that a submarine *had* got in, then the first explosion—twelve minutes before the others—must have represented a bare hit right up in the bow from a salvo of three or four. Where were the missing two or three torpedoes? And if they had struck the rocks and exploded, why had no one heard? Those would have been really visible audible explosions—unlike the muffled internal-sounding thumps which had sunk the *Royal Oak*. More curious still, assuming the explosion in the Inflammable Store to be a torpedo hit on the bow, then it had hit by a margin of a few feet only and the other torpedoes in the salvo had missed completely. As the *Royal Oak* was lying with her starboard side to the land, then the submarine must have fired from less than half a mile away at a huge, stationary target—and missed it. Even those who had heard "Pony" Moore say that he could bring in a submarine through Kirk Sound thought that this particular affair had nothing to do with submarines.

The men were equally depressed; most of them were convinced that the explosions had been internal, and they thought they knew what had caused them. Marine Owens believed that, while swimming with a midshipman, he had seen the conning tower, and part of the hull of a submarine a hundred yards away. However, it was a dark night, it might easily have been an optical illusion, possibly the gig floating upside down with a man astride the keel. "Sabotage" was the virtually unanimous conclusion. Paradoxically and illogically, proof that they had been torpedoed would improve morale one hundred per cent. Sabotage, it was felt, could occur anywhere, any time, whereas if a submarine had got through some gap, then the gap could be closed. In the circumstances, a submarine it had to be, whether it was or not.

During the morning—it was still Saturday the 14th—the Admiralty announced that the *Royal Oak* had been lost, "believed by U-boat action," and issued the first fifteen names of survivors. At the same time, they ordered an immediate concentration of divers at Scapa Flow. The battleship lay bottom up but heeled over partly onto her starboard side in about one hundred feet of water, so that at low tide her port bilges showed above the surface. A Fleet Air Arm pilot, who had just flown over her, came into the dormitory at Hatston airdrome where Cleverley was, and told them that the *Royal Oak* had "four big holes in her that you could drive a bus through."

An examination of those holes would soon prove whether the explosions had been internal or external; further, if she had been sunk by torpedoes, undeniable proof, in the shape of bits of them, would be lying around waiting to be picked up. The parts, if they were there, would also be of interest to the Admiralty's Torpedo Experimental Establishment at Greenock. But, if the minesweepers could find a complete, unexploded torpedo, that would be even better. The missing torpedoes were never found, either then or later.

The news of the sinking was reported in B.B.C. news bulletins late in the morning, and repeated. The statement that fifteen survivors had been landed was taken by many anxious relatives to mean that there had been *only* fifteen. Afternoon newspapers carried the story on their front pages, under flaring headlines—apart from the *Courageous*, it was the first big-ship loss—and gave the names of the fifteen. This was all the news they had; they filled in with statistics, history of the ship, and the last-known list of senior officers. The Germans picked up the continual B.B.C. announcements and began to repeat them, adding that nothing about the operation was yet known in Germany. In the dockyard towns, particularly Portsmouth, where most of the men came from, crowds of friends and relatives gathered outside the Royal Naval Barracks to read the names as, hourly, fresh lists of survivors were put up. Most of them would not read there the name they hoped to see.

Mrs. Parham, wife of the Sergeant gunnery instructor, did not turn on the radio that day. The B.B.C., geared to total war from the start, had liberally studded their program plans with spaces for news announcements; those spaces had to be filled, whether or not there was any new news. People soon got tired of listening. During the afternoon Mrs. Parham did not go out, so missed seeing the newspaper placards shouting *"Royal Oak* Sunk." When a neighbor, who worked in the commander in chief's office, called to say, "Your husband's safe," Mrs. Parham had no idea what she was talking about.

On the other hand, even before the first announcement, Mrs. Booth, worried by her dream, tried to tell her mother about it. All she got was a refusal even to listen, on the grounds that a "Friday night dream on a Saturday told" is bad luck. "Well, he's safe, anyway!" she shouted at her mother's retreating back. At midday her sister came in with the news that the *Royal Oak* had gone, so she went with her baby son to Eastney Barracks to look at the lists of names. Her husband's name was not there. Anything might have happened, even a battle, for the Admiralty announcement made no mention of where or in what circumstances the battleship had been lost.

Mrs. Walker, with two sons in the Navy, had also had a dream that night. She had awakened her husband to say that she had dreamed of newsboys in the streets shouting, "Loss of the *Royal Oak*." Their youngest son, Cecil Edward Walker, aged sixteen, was serving in her. For Mrs. Walker there was to be no name on a survivors' list.

Another mother of a sixteen-year-old son, Bugler Harry Mountford, R.M., had at his request pleaded with the Drum Major to let him go to sea. She thought at the time that it meant only a two-year commission in the Mediterranean. He, too, was dead.

In the *Voltaire*, all that day, there were roll calls; name after name read out, and no answer.

Almost all the boys had gone, except for a proportion of those in the battery. The Admiral was dead and the Gunnery Officer, Lieutenant Commander Roper, with his second-in-command, "Pony" Moore; so was Captain Edgar Balls, commanding the Royal Marines detachment. From Portsmouth alone, there were more than forty Marines lost. The stokers had suffered particularly badly and the Maltese mess had been almost wiped out. Three of the men landed by the *Daisy* were dead on arrival or died shortly after; one of the wounded, Stoker Tate, was soon to die. Only a third of the ship's company remained. Twenty-four officers and 809 men had lost their lives.

In the *Voltaire*, a container of rum was broached; anyone who wanted to help himself could do so. For some survivors that was the highlight of the whole affair; but a surprisingly large number did not drink. That night, in the hospital ship, few of the badly burned men slept much, even when doped; it was the first sleepless night in an endless succession of tormented nights and days.

"Several of us wore a bandage mask on our faces," wrote Petty Officer Kerr, while the memory was still vivid. "There were two holes to see through and a slit for the mouth. Our mouths were swelled and blistered, the same as our faces, and all we kept on wanting was fluid to wet the mouth. We couldn't sleep with our pain and thoughts, and used to long for the morning to come. The night sister gave us shots of morphia that killed the pain for a while and we could sleep; but not for long, as I used to have the most terrifying dreams of that tragic morning. The doctor asked me one night how I felt, I expect he saw tears in my eyes, they were there, I know; I told him I could not help thinking about my old shipmates. He patted me on the shoulder and said, 'Try to get some sleep.'"

The padre, who looked after the patients' library, went round giving out books to the less badly injured. "You would have thought," said Surgeon Commander Delisle Gray, "that these lads who had just looked death right between his eyes would have chosen some quiet, unexciting books. Nothing of the sort. They all, without exception, chose the most lurid murder and adventure stories they could find!"

On Sunday, the 15th, diving operations began. What the divers found there echoes still. There were bodies leaning out of the wreck, half in and half out of the portholes; there were corpses in the hull, jammed by falling gear; and on the sea bed, the bloated shapes of drowned swimmers floated more or less upright, executing in the tides a macabre undersea dance.

The bottom was of sand and such clouds arose, whenever a diver moved foot or hand, that they had to enter the riven darkness of the hull and work there in that mass tomb by touch alone. One of the divers, a Portsmouth man, had had a son in the *Royal Oak;* he was still in the hull. The father was not required to dive, but helped supervise from the surface. The scenes found below were still being passed on among the Orkney Defense Force years afterwards; it was said that divers had come up, crazed with horror.

But apart from this, the divers did not talk. There was a security blanket on the work, which still lingers. Metal Industries (Salvage) Ltd., whose divers took part, as late as November, 1958, politely referred a request for information to the Admiralty. The diving boat, the survivors heard, was manned entirely by officers. H.M.S. *Vernon,* the Navy's mine and diving establishment, supplied a large contingent. One of these men told a survivor, later, that he was flown up for the work, that he carried out one dive, made his report, was immediately flown back to Portsmouth, and two days afterwards flown out to Libya. Even if he did talk, no one diver could possibly re-create anything like a complete picture of the wreck or of the damage to it; for that, he would need to talk to other divers. Only on the basis of reports from many divers, working simultaneously on and around the hull, could a plan and, eventually, a model of the wreck be made.

Some information did leak, in due course, but to survivors only; unfortunately it was contradictory. Diver H. told one survivor that he had found pieces of torpedo down there; Diver W. told one survivor, and the wife of another, that he had found no traces of torpedo, that the plates were blown outwards, as from internal explosion, and that "you could drive a double-decker bus through the hole." Even nineteen years afterwards, these men would not be interviewed.

While this work, wrapped in strictest secrecy, went on, a

simultaneous survey was being made of the fixed defenses of Scapa Flow. There was no evidence to show that a submarine had got through the booms at Hoxa Sound, Switha Sound or Hoy Sound. Surveys were then made of the eastern entrances closed by blockships; particular attention was paid to Kirk Sound, about which the dead Lieutenant Moore had made an official report. The channel was in fact navigable by surface vessels and in use by them; but a submarine, extremely hard to handle in a high-speed current bubbling round corners, which was the position here except at slack water, would be likely to strike a blockship and leave traces.

Chief Petty Officer E. G. Pratt, a naval pensioner called up a few months before, took part in the survey of Kirk Sound. Curiously enough, he, like McLaverty, had been in Scapa Flow when the *Vanguard* blew up, and remembered it vividly. While other people took soundings at high and low water, he got on with his job—which was to examine the blockships for any sign that a submarine had got through and grazed them in its passing, as it was very likely to do. He returned a nil report—"Not a barnacle scratched off 'em."

While the surveys were still going on a blockship arrived at Scapa—it was intended for Kirk Sound. It was a replacement for a blockship sent earlier, which had been sunk during its passage to Orkney. Even if it had got there, it would still have arrived after the outbreak of war; this was due partly to protracted negotiations with the Treasury, but only partly. The best outlay for the strictly limited amount of money available to them, was the responsibility of the Admiralty.

About two dozen bodies had been recovered from the Flow, indicating that the number drowned had been smaller than had at first appeared likely and that most of the 833 men lost had died inside the ship, while still trying to get out. Some of the two dozen even might have floated out of the wreck; and it was subsequently reported that nets had been placed over it to prevent this happening.

The dead men were brought to Lyness and a number of survivors were asked to identify them. Some, with a horror of recognizing friends, refused to do it; Batterbury was one. But Sergeant Booth took part—the first man he saw was a senior engineer; Farley took part—an ordnance artificer friend was lying there. All, said Farley, had died by drowning, there were no external wounds. On Monday, the 16th, they were buried in the naval cemetery at Lyness, among the crosses of the men who had died in the *Vanguard* and of Germans from the surrendered High Seas Fleet.

It was a cold, sunny day. As the long lines of survivors followed a bugler and a squad of ratings with rifles at the trail up the hill above Lyness, the sun was momentarily obscured by a passing cloud. Two men in the leading file of survivors carried wreaths; behind them marched a motley array, few of whom were properly dressed. Mostly, they wore boiler suits and white gym shoes, issued in the *Voltaire;* many had white caps instead of black; some were wearing clothes given to them by the crews of the *Daisy* and the *Pegasus.* As the funeral party stood with reversed arms above the graves and the bugle notes rang over the hill, the sun, directly behind the ranks, shone out and cast their shadows across the raw earth.

During the day, news came in of an air raid on that part of the Home Fleet which was lying in the Firth of Forth, one of its alternative bases; the cruiser *Southampton* was hit by a bomb which did not explode and the destroyer *Mohawk* was damaged by splinters. Most of the heavy units were at another alternative base, Loch Ewe.

In the *Voltaire,* arrangements were being made to hold a Court of Enquiry next day; Vice-Admiral R. H. T. Raikes had come to Scapa to conduct it. Statements had been taken from key witnesses. Cleverley, still at the airdrome, had not been able to say much, except that he thought it was sabotage—which was not well received; Fossey had been interviewed by half a dozen officers who seemed to know a lot about it already. Captain Benn did not show himself much to the ratings in the *Voltaire;* for him the tragedy had been a crushing blow. At one moment he had been in command of a 29,000-ton battleship, the next he was unemployed, and likely to remain so if the verdict of the Court went against him. But he made a point of visiting the wounded in the *Aba.* Fossey was the last man he came to in that particular ward; he asked if Fossey, who had been on watch, had seen the submarine. "That shook me," said Fossey, "it was the first thing I'd heard about a submarine; and I don't think to this day it was." After Captain Benn had gone, a buzz of excited talk broke out in the ward; this theory was new to them, too.

The gospel of a submarine was intensively spread by the officers, whatever their private thoughts; they publicly ridiculed all suggestions of sabotage. At this time, the minesweepers had recovered nothing—and never would do so —while the divers were investigating with such secrecy that, if the answer should be unwelcome, in the sense of being damaging to morale, it would never be known.

That evening an impromptu concert was organized in the *Voltaire,* to cheer people up; and the audience insisted on singing "Daisy, Daisy" as a mark of gratitude to Skipper Gatt and his crew. In the *Aba,* another tormented night began for the badly burned men.

Next day, Tuesday the 17th, Sergeant Booth went over to the *Iron Duke* for mail; he had asked to do this duty because his brother-in-law, a chief supply rating, was in her. The mail office was on her quarter-deck, in place of "Y" turret, which had been removed when she was demilitarized. There was a bag of mail for the *Royal Oak* and Booth collected this. While he was away, Blundell was in the well deck of the *Voltaire* with a party rigging it up for the Court of Enquiry; Lieutenant Benton was outside his cabin. Blundell heard the usual air raid warning "Red." Then he heard aircraft engines; he had never heard them before, the German reconnaissance aircraft always flew too high. But these sounded loud enough and the planes seemed to be diving. Then he saw them—three Heinkel 111s coming down in a long shallow dive at the ships in the Flow. Benton heard the whining roar of diving planes, then the stutter of machine guns. "Christ, this it it!" he thought, and ran on deck. Planes were going down on the *Iron Duke*, and more were coming in over the Flow, and starting to dive.

Blundell saw two bombs fall from the second Heinkel towards the *Iron Duke;* they looked about the size of sea-bags and they were jerking as they fell. An enormous wall of water rose up close alongside the battleship's stern and then subsided onto her quarter-deck—what might have been either bodies or mailbags went with it, when it poured back into the sea.

The *Aba,* much nearer to the *Iron Duke* than the *Voltaire,* seemed to be directly under the attacking planes. "It was horrible," said Finley, "because if the ship was hit, we were done, we couldn't do a thing about it." A nurse stood beside Finley all the time, holding his hand, to calm him; she never flinched. Bendell, highly excited, scrambled out of his cot to a port, and began to shout a commentary. "Look—here's another one coming down!" The rising metallic howl of aircraft engines passed over the hospital ship. "Oh, they hit her that time!" More and more aircraft thundered over, beginning their dives from directly above the patients in the ward. All the A.A. guns were firing, and the high-pitched detonations mixed with the gutteral throb of engines and the whine of the diving aircraft. High above the racket rose the shrill, rising whistle of descending bombs, increasing to a howling shriek, and dissolving in the roar of explosions.

A ward sister dashed in, dragged Bendell away from the port, and put him back to bed.

A little group, including Lieutenant Keen, were leaning on the rails of the *Voltaire*, watching the attack with great interest—it was their first air raid and the barrage seemed to them fairly impressive. They saw the *Iron Duke* half hidden, time and again, by huge bursts of white spray; they saw her heel over increasingly and begin to sink by the stern; with a slightly self-conscious air of bravado and superior knowledge they began to compare the list she was now taking on with a similar stage in the sinking of the *Royal Oak*.

Booth was in the *Iron Duke*, at first on her quarterdeck and then, when the buzzers sounded the alarm, down below under "X" turret with a cup of rum given him by a chief stoker whom he had known in the light cruiser *Durban*. There were two violent detonations, the main steam pipe cracked, bits fell off all over the place, the deck was obscured by steam, water began to come in, and the ship took on that familiar, increasing list. Booth was straight up on deck within seconds, asked permission to abandon ship, and went straight over the side, hanging on to his mailbag.

As he swam away, more planes were coming in at the *Iron Duke*, which was heeling right over to port, her guns still firing. Booth saw a gun crew fall away from a gun, after another bomb explosion; he saw a Marine run to an abandoned pom-pom and open fire. Bullets lashed the water among the swimmers—he was not the only one to have abandoned ship—and some of them disappeared in the old, familiar manner. Bombs were scattering the sea around the *Aba*—he saw her go over and then come back again, apparently undamaged. Within minutes a fishing boat picked him up, the crew gave him a sheepskin coat, and then set him on the shore at Lyness, a few hundred yards away. He set off away from the Flow, carrying the sodden bag of mail.

Lieutenant Benton, in charge of a boat from the *Voltaire*, put away to pick up survivors from the *Iron Duke;* and swarms of small craft, virtually everything afloat in the area, began to converge on her. Acting as tugs, they closed the heeling battleship and began to push and pull at her sides with the object of beaching her before she sank. The bombers were still coming, and every gun that would fire was blazing away, even the colliers joined in. The fire was ragged, inaccurate and highly dangerous to all concerned, friend and foe alike.

From the deck of the *Voltaire* Saltmarsh was gazing fascinated at the big bombers diving down through the bursting black puffs of A.A. fire, the black crosses visible on wings and fuselage, and at the fountains of water shooting up from the Flow and then subsiding again. He saw the *Iron Duke* heel over amid columns of spray, and as the mailbags rolled off her deck a terrific roar of disappointment came from the rest of the *Royal Oak*'s survivors.

He saw one plane pull away from a bombing run on the battleship, the target of every gun that would bear. It suddenly fell away towards the interior of Hoy and went down behind a hill. Instantly a pillar of black smoke billowed up from the spot. Then, looking upwards, he could see a parachute, tiny and white in the distance, drifting im-

perceptibly downwards—there was a roar of cheering from
the decks of the *Voltaire*. Slowly, the red sparks of tracer
bullets began to climb up towards the man hanging under
the parachute, and there was another savage cheer from
the *Voltaire;* Saltmarsh felt sick.

The Fleet minesweeper *Hebe* claimed to have hit the
aircraft with a three-inch "brick"; a boom defense vessel
commanded by an officer known as the "Purple Emperor"
claimed it, too; no one could really tell. But it was down all
right, falling directly ahead of Sergeant Booth, trudging
inland with his sodden mailbag. Having "seen enough
carnage already," he altered course at once, and ran
straight into the arms of a naval patrol sent out to bring
in any surviving air crew. What they saw was a man
dressed in blue overalls, with a sheepskin coat which
looked like a pilot's, trudging away from the scene of the
crash.

They closed in on Booth and began to march him, under guard, back to Lyness. Booth, having just made his
second "ditching" from a sinking battleship, was not especially coherent. It was not until after several minutes'
interrogation at Lyness that the Navy regretfully decided
he was "one of ours," and put him into the *Iron Duke's*
cutter, still holding the mailbag.

By now the aircraft were flying back across the Pentland
Firth and the *Iron Duke,* badly holed below the waterline
by two near misses, was steadily being pushed by the
horde of small craft towards the northern shore of Longhope, a few hundred yards away. Pumps were quite unable
to control the water pouring into her and she went to the
bottom at last, technically "sunk," but upright in the shal-
lows. And there she remained, with a concrete bottom and
the water pumped out, for the rest of the war, still acting
as depot ship.

A new patient was brought out to the *Aba*—the German who had come down by parachute, the only survivor from the aircraft. As often happens in these cases, with the best will in the world, the machine gunners had missed him. He was suffering from burns and broken ribs.

In case of further raids, the Captain of the *Voltaire* "cleared lower deck" of all *Royal Oak* survivors; they were taken in boats to the island of Flotta, a few hundred yards away, and told to scatter. Their dinner would be brought to them. Lieutenant Benton came back from returning *Iron Duke* survivors to the *Iron Duke,* to be pressed at once into this service. He was returning from his final trip, closely followed by another boat of which Sergeant Mc-Laverty was in charge, when air raid warning "Red" sounded again. "Christ," he thought, "I know what that means—the bar's going to close." And it did.

"It was a fascinating experience," said Leading Telegraphist Jones, "to watch the Ju 88 squadrons come over in groups of nine at 12,000 feet in a bright blue sky. We could hear their engines long in advance, it was so quiet. We could see the bombs leave the aircraft in sticks and see the ships being straddled." Batterbury was able to resist the fascination of the spectacle sufficiently to put his head down in the heather, out of the way of the splinters flying about. When he found that the heather was not heather, but the decomposing intestines of a long-dead sheep, he still kept it there.

"It was beautiful bombing," said Lieutenant Keen, "but the luck was dead against them." A destroyer began to get under way and, as she gathered speed, a stick landed where she had been; another stick straddled the *Aba,* another landed between the *Voltaire* and a collier, yet another straddled the boom. McLaverty's boat ran right into the stick aimed for the *Voltaire* and a waterspout leaped up a few hundred yards away. He let go of the tiller and the four rowers dropped the oars, while they lay flat; when they popped their heads up again, they had lost their means of locomotion and steerage until the "Green Parrot," the Admiral's barge from the *Iron Duke*, took them in tow.

Surgeon Commander Delisle Gray was in the saloon of the *Aba*, finishing lunch, when the attack began. Through the scuttles the officers there clearly saw the flash of a bomb explosion and heard the fragments rattle along the sides of the hospital ship.

"I jumped up from table and ran into the surgical ward, which was next to the dining saloon. There I found the forty injured men lying quietly in their cots. Not a man moved. The ward Sister went on doing the dressings as if nothing was happening. I walked around and spoke to a few of the lads and to a Marine (not from the *Royal Oak*), who had a fractured thigh. He was in a Thomas splint, with the splint lashed to the end of the cot. He pointed to his foot and said, 'What's to happen to me, sir?' I put my hand in my trouser pocket, took out my knife, and said, 'I put this in my pocket specially for you during the first raid. If anything happens to the ship I shall cut you adrift and you shall be the first man out of the ward.' Meanwhile forty pairs of eyes were fixed on me and followed me wherever I went.

"A friend of the Marine then went up to him, felt his chin, and said, 'You haven't shaved this morning.' He got some hot water, stropped the razor, lathered him up, and shaved him, while the bombs were dropping around us. Truly the British service-man has the guts of a lion."

The battleship's cutter, in all this, was still heading for Flotta with Sergeant Booth and his mailbag; he saw cascades of water shoot up all round the boom and had the impression that one of the bar boats virtually became airborne, the waterspouts leading inexorably to the cutter. "For Christ's sake, Coxswain," he yelled, "alter course, they're coming right for us!"

"Who's coxswain?" replied the Coxswain.

On that, the next stick came whining down and Booth went through the air, still clutching the mailbag, for his third "ditching" in four days. He swam the rest of the way to Flotta. As he crawled out of the water he met Captain Benn, who said, "What—not you, too?"

The German unit concerned in these two attacks was the Hinkelbein Gruppe of the Adler Geschwader, led by Lieutenant Colonel Loebel. A Gruppe was roughly equivalent to an R.A.F. Wing, and consisted of thirty bombers. They were not opposed by fighters, except some invisible aircraft sent up afterwards by excited pressmen. The low-performance Navy fighters could not intercept and there were no R.A.F. fighters based anywhere near. The Luftwaffe publication, *Adler Jahrbuch*, claimed a "deadly blow." It was hardly that, although they had certainly inflicted far more damage than they had received; they had also done far better than had Bomber Command in its attacks on German warships more heavily defended by flak, which was hardly surprising. The Intelligence "tip-off" that an air attack on Scapa Flow was impending had been proved correct; their estimate of the numbers which would be involved had been totally wrong, their figure should have been divided by twenty. But the most surprising thing was that the Luftwaffe, like the R.A.F., were trying to sink warships by throwing tiddlywinks at them some fifteen years after "Billy" Mitchell, to the fury of the United States Navy and his own professional ruin, had smuggled four-thousand-pound bombs into his aircraft and promptly

put target warships of the same vintage as the *Iron Duke*
on the bottom. It was not until Pearl Harbor that the ad-
vocates of the airplane came into their own.

The bombing did achieve one definite thing, however—
it got the survivors home quickly. Captain Benn was heard
speaking on the telephone in the *Voltaire,* apparently lay-
ing down the law to the Admiralty, insisting that his men
had had enough of it, and had to be taken away. Just before dark they were taken off Flotta by the minesweepers
Hebe and *Britomart,* and disembarked at Scrabster, the
port of Thurso, about six P.M.; and after dark the *Aba* got
under way for Invergordon.

At least two survivors were better dressed in consequence. Paymaster Commander Cundall, in the hospital
ship, was loaned a complete uniform by the padre, who
would not, however, include a collar in the loan. In the
Hebe, Batterbury was given a pair of sailor's trousers with
the right leg missing, an improvement on what he was
wearing. McLaverty was still stuck with overalls and two
left boots, "big, gravel-punching Marine's boots."

They were taken into Thurso and billeted, at very short
notice indeed, in the homes of many kindly people. Mrs.
B. Gunn opened the door of her house, that dark winter's
night, to see two men there, one of whom was Stanley Saltmarsh. "Stanley," she said, "was shivering in an old rain-
coat, vest and pants, with a pair of sandals on his feet. The
other man was more decently clad, but the supply had run
down. Stanley was violently sick and sort of delirious owing
to the oil he had swallowed in the sea. Next morning I got
gray pants and a pullover off my son and a brother-in-law
supplied a warm jacket. Stanley has never forgotten and
I still get a card from him at Christmas."

None of the other survivors forgot, either. "They stripped
their wardrobes for us," was the general comment. Booth,

who had no shoes, was given slippers, plus a pair of fisher-
man's trousers and a tam-o-shanter, or "balmoral." One
man, before leaving, was given a cake for the journey
home, and found a ten shilling note underneath it. The
way they were looked after by the Port Commander, known
to them only as "Peg-Leg Joe," matched that of the inhabitants; "He was a real gentleman," said Parham.

Petty Officer Kennedy, Acting Petty Officer Blundell,
Able Seaman Ayles, and another man were billeted together. They settled down, after food, to listen to the radio.
As was normal in Britain at that time they tuned in to the
enemy for light relief and diversion from the B.B.C. At
9:15, said Blundell, they heard a man announced as Lieutenant Gunther Prien. He spoke in English. His U-boat had
that day returned to Germany, after entering Scapa Flow,
sinking the *Royal Oak* and damaging the *Repulse*. "He
spoke from Kiel," recalled Blundell. "He didn't give any
details of how he got into the Flow. He said he could
clearly see a battleship and a two-funneled battle cruiser,
clearly silhouetted against the bright moonlit sky. And, although he spoke for five or ten minutes, that sentence was
the only one that sticks out in my mind. I remember Kennedy and I looking at one another and saying, 'The ruddy
liar.'

"It was pitch black and cloudy; he couldn't have seen us
from the distance he said he fired. As cox of the picket
boat, I know that. There was a two-funneled battle cruiser
near us in the morning, at the time the reconnaissance
plane came over; the Germans wouldn't know that it left
harbor a few hours later. The U-boat story was cooked; it
wasn't there."

12

"Blimey, Where's Snow White?"

The sinking of the *Royal Oak*, as yet by "an unknown agency," on the 14th, the damaging of the *Southampton* and *Mohawk* by air attack in the Firth of Forth on the 16th, the technical "sinking" of the *Iron Duke* in the first of the two Scapa air raids on the 17th, as well as previous attempts to lure warships into bomber and U-boat traps, made it clear that the Home Fleet was the target of a planned campaign designed to achieve by degrees what the Japanese were later to visit on the United States Navy in one overwhelming blow. Clearly, further attacks were imminent.

The First Lord of the Admiralty (Winston Churchill) reacted with characteristic sweep and vigor; on the 18th he reported to the Cabinet that Scapa Flow must be for the moment abandoned as a fleet anchorage and decided that Loch Ewe on the west coast of Scotland, which was hardly defended at all, would be the alternative base. In so doing he reacted exactly as the shrewd Germans anticipated and went straight into the trap, liberally studded with magnetic mines, which they proceeded to lay for him.

He did not get his way without protest because, to any-one not obsessed with doing something regardless, even Scapa seemed better than Loch Ewe; and Rosyth, too, was vulnerable to mines. If the *Royal Oak* had been sunk by a U-boat the measures required were small—a few more req-uisitioned fishing drifters to patrol the entrances, or some lengths of cable, or a better watch, or a few small-caliber guns; if she had been sunk by explosives placed in the stores then the searching of stores before they were loaded would suffice (the survivors heard at Thurso that this was being done). But the last attack had been air attack and, although only thirty bombers had appeared instead of the eight hundred predicted, it was air attack which loomed largest. The simple thought that the Germans might ring the changes, to keep everyone on the hop, was not suffi-ciently considered.

Ring the changes they did, by air and sea mining; and the results were soon apparent. On November 21st the brand new cruiser *Belfast* became a total loss in the Firth of Forth and on December 4th the battleship *Nelson,* flag-ship of Admiral Forbes, had an eighty-foot hole torn in her bow by a mine laid in the entrance to Loch Ewe. The losses were mounting, although some were kept secret. The *Nelson* went to Portsmouth for repairs and the Germans got wind of it. The Admiralty hate telling a lie and will go to great lengths of grammatical ingenuity to avoid doing so. They did not deny the German claim, they merely said that it was "too ridiculous to deny."

At Thurso, the Court of Enquiry into the sinking of the *Royal Oak* had begun on October 18th. Forms were handed out to all survivors, with a standard set of ques-tions to be answered: (a) where were you at the time of the first—second—third—fourth explosions? (b) how many explosions did you hear? (c) did you see any flash, fire, smoke? (d) how did you get away? (e) who else was with you?

The results of these enquiries—diving operations and inspection of the entrances still continued—were never publicly divulged. Captain Roskill, the official historian, later skated delicately and with apparent naïveté over the whole question in two revealing sentences:

> Meanwhile inside the Flow it was realised that a U-boat had probably penetrated the defences, but a search by every available vessel revealed no trace of her. *Such doubts as might still remain* were dispelled a few days later when the enemy announced Prien's success. . . .*

The onus of publicly stating that it was a U-boat was thrown onto the narrow shoulders of Dr. Goebbels; his word was accepted without question, although he was gleefully capable of faking a U-boat into Scapa Flow and faking it out again and had, within hours of the sinking, kindly been given the hint by the Admiralty through B.B.C. announcements. Indeed, it was only a few weeks since he had faked a Polish attack on a German frontier post, complete with real, bullet-riddled corpses for the edification of newspapermen. In fact, the Admiralty were keeping an open mind on what had sunk the *Royal Oak*, but the German claim was a gift from the gods, as far as morale was concerned.

Among the survivors there was great relief at the news; many of them accepted it completely. Leading Telegraphist Jones cynically observed that if the defenses of Scapa were anything like the rest of the war effort, any U-boat

* *The War at Sea*, Vol. I. *My italics.*

could get in any time it wanted. Which was perfectly true.
Other survivors were spending their evenings in pubs trying to work out, with local skippers, whether a U-boat
could get in and out again in the time allowed, and then
return to Germany in time for Prien to broadcast from
Kiel. The broadcast, which was reported in the British
press on the 19th, hardly inspired confidence. It was pre-
recorded and the following extracts were published:

> It was quite a job to smuggle ourselves into Scapa
> Flow through all the British defences. I saw two British
> warships to the north of me, and discharged two tor-
> pedoes at them. I at once turned my boat and left the
> harbour, because I did not want my ship and crew to be
> captured. As I left the port I heard two explosions and
> saw a column of water rising from the British ship lying
> farthest north. A moment later the other ship exploded.
> I saw parts of her blown into the air and then the whole
> ship disappeared. Then I realised that the northern ship
> was seriously damaged too—she had two funnels, which
> proves she was not the *Royal Oak*. Just as we were leav-
> ing the port intense activity began there. The surface of
> the sea was lit by searchlights, and several depth charges
> exploded behind us. You cannot imagine how cheerful
> and happy I felt when, a few minutes later, a thundering
> cheer sounded over the sea from my crew.

Prien gave a press conference, which was also reported
in the British press. He told much the same amazing story
as before, with the following additions:

> I saw straight in front of me the outline of two large
> warships. The first torpedo struck the boat with two

funnels, which was the further away of the two vessels. The second torpedo struck the ship lying nearer to us. As this partly screened the further ship, our first torpedo could only be aimed at the visible portion. It therefore struck the ship forward, as a result of which the vessel —I am speaking of the *Repulse*—was considerably damaged, the bows, as we established beyond dispute, sinking deep into the water. The effect of the second torpedo was queer. Several columns of water rose high from the ship's sides, and columns of fire were visible in all the colours of the rainbow. Bits of wreckage were hurled through the air. They were fragments of the funnel, masts, and bridge. It was my aim not only to sink a British ship in a British Naval harbour, but also to keep my crew and boat for further tasks. We went out the same way as we had come in. Behind us great activity with searchlights and Morse signalling began.

As a result of this farrago of nonsense, the Germans were claiming that the *Repulse* had been damaged, as well as the *Royal Oak* sunk. When Petty Officer Kerr was sufficiently recovered to read these accounts he wrote in a scrapbook he was keeping of the affair:

Although the fifteen of us in hospital with multiple burns curse the U-boat for sinking our ship and killing 800 of our shipmates, we all say it was a courageous feat of seamanship of remarkable skill and daring, also the captain of her was a hero and a gentleman. But the stories published by the German press (the two reports just quoted) are all false claims, which makes it seem that the U-boat crew that was decorated by Admiral Raeder was for propaganda purposes and they never saw the inside of Scapa.

Submarine commanders' reports frequently are very in-accurate, particularly as regards night operations, but Pri-en's account went far beyond what might reasonably be allowed. One cannot damage a ship which is not there, or mistake a single-funneled ship for a two-funneled one, or mistake west for north, or imagine nonexistent searchlights and depth charges. On all counts bar one the story was a fake. There were those curious repeated references to his withdrawal from Scapa, as though he were somehow ashamed of it.

Certainly the Admiralty were not taking it for gospel, al-though they affected to do so. A proportion only of the survivors were interviewed, after the forms had been checked; many of them must have been unsatisfactory. The men were fed up and, literally, far from home; they wanted to get away on leave. Others were intimidated by the array of rank, said "Yessir" and "Nosir" where re-quired, and got out thankfully. Others again found that both fire and flash were frowned upon, the interviewers seemed to want not to believe it. Chief Engine-room Artifi-cer Wilson, who had boldly written "Internal explosions" on his form, was told, shortly, "Tripe." When Able Seaman Farley got in, they unbent sufficiently to argue the point. A torpedo, it was pointed out to him, traveled at some speed and might reasonably be expected to penetrate the hull before exploding. Farley said, afterwards, "I didn't wear that."

What that speed would be was a matter entirely of con-jecture, unless or until sufficient fragments were found to reconstruct it. Twenty-six knots would be the probable speed, but there were rumors of German torpedoes of the trackless type capable of fifty knots, though they would not have said as much to Farley. On the other hand Stoker Cleverley, if he had been there, could have testified that the third explosion lifted the armored deck in the cross-passage between the mess decks, almost on the center line of the ship. That presupposed a torpedo sufficiently fast and a warhead sufficiently powerful to penetrate both the antitorpedo bulges and several small compartments and then blow open the armored deck, designed to keep out bombs and plunging fire from big guns, and so put Cleverley in hospital for nearly four weeks with flash burns. It really was a bit hard to believe. But if a container about the size of a torpedo warhead had been introduced into the Central Stores, which were somewhat on the starboard side but inboard, approximately where that explosion seemed to have occurred, then it would have produced just those results which had been brought so violently to Cleverley's notice. Additionally, Finley who was at the time directly above that point, but several decks higher, had been cut down at the precise moment of the third explosion by what appeared to be the flash from it. Unlike those aft of the stokers' mess decks, who had been burned by an unmistakable cordite flame venting near the night "heads," Finley had been hit by an almost instantaneous flash traveling upwards, as the nature of his injuries indicated.

The Germans were suspected to possess, although there was no proof of its use so far, a magnetic fuse for use with torpedoes (technically known as a "noncontact pistol"). Instead of striking the protected sides of a major warship, it would be set to run deep and explode directly under the hull, the most vulnerable point of all. Such an explosion would be unlikely to produce a waterspout and probably would give the impression of being internal; but it was unlikely to be used in the shallow waters of an anchorage. It is doubtful if it would have produced the results seen by Cleverley and it could not have cut down Finley.

When Leading Supply Assistant Sims was interviewed,

the word "tripe" was not used in connection with his belief that the explosions had been internal; far from it. The interviewers were most interested in anyone who could tell them precisely what had been put into the storerooms on the previous day; indeed he was a "key" witness. "It was a long interview," recalled Sims, "awkward questions, all about storing ship—the packages, how packed, anything suspicious. They thought there might have been a bomb planted in the food."

Sims did not think so. He replied that the containers were mostly about 2½ x 1½ x 1½ feet, weighing perhaps half a hundredweight. The bomb could not possibly have come in the guise of victuals; the packages were too small and too light. His suspicions of sabotage were based on the muffled nature of the explosions, as they had seemed to him, and the strange gaps between them; he had no idea where they had occurred.

On the other hand Sergeant Booth, who had been in charge of the Marine working party helping with the stores, recalled that five forty-gallon drums of oil had been loaded from a lighter towed alongside by the *Daisy*. They were certainly heavy, he had lifted one, and they were about the size of a torpedo warhead. One he thought had been stowed forward in the CO_2, near the Inflammable Store, three had gone into the Central Stores amidships, and the last had been stowed in the after tiller area. In other words, more or less exactly where the explosions had occurred.

But if the explosions had in fact been sabotage that postulated a quite elaborate effort on the part of some person or persons unknown, which was disturbing to think about. In the first world war the Germans had destroyed quite a number of ships sailing from American ports by placing time bombs in them; but these were merchant ships and the bombs were really incendiaries. Placed in the cargo by an agent acting as a stevedore, they set fire to it, and that was that; quite a small bomb would do the trick. To destroy a 29,000-ton battleship by explosion was a totally different matter.

In a major warship, a small bomb would work only if introduced into a magazine; the magazines were the best guarded parts of the ship and two of the explosions, at least, had been nowhere near a magazine. Besides a magazine explosion would be likely to set off a shell room and that would destroy the ship almost instantaneously, would produce in fact a second *Vanguard*. Prien's description of the sinking—"fragments of the funnel, mast and bridge . . . hurled through the air"—although, curiously enough, having a more than passable likeness to the *Vanguard* affair, bore no relation whatever to the sinking of the *Royal Oak*. No main magazine had exploded, still less a shell room, although some magazine, and that probably small, had vented and produced a cordite flame. As the divers were now finding out, the only magazine which had been wrecked, possibly by explosion, was a small-arms magazine.

A considerable quantity of high explosive must have been put in the ship, disguised as stores; furthermore, it could not have been added casually to the other stores as a surplus item, or there would have been questions from the supply staff. If it had been in the oil drums, then the drums must have been carefully prepared, because a solid-sounding oil drum would at once excite suspicion. And, at some point, the four or five items of doctored stores must have been "switched" for similar stores already on the invoices. Granted that that could have been done, the rest was easy; new stores would be opened last, and it was unlikely that anyone would touch them in the few hours that remained before the time mechanisms worked. Those mechanisms would not be clockwork; at that stage of the war they were likely to be acid, and doubly likely to be unreliable, producing awkward gaps between explosions quite unlike the ten- or fifteen-second intervals of a submarine putting over her helm to produce a torpedo "spread."

There would, too, have been plenty of advance warning of the storing operation. Before the *Royal Oak* entered Scapa, stores would have been demanded from a large number of departments, so that a great many people would know that a worthwhile target, a battleship, was due to store on a given day; and the stores would be waiting for her when she arrived. It was common talk among the survivors that some of the stores had been lying unguarded for twenty-four hours on Lyness jetty, stenciled with the *Royal Oak*'s name.

The ideal agent would be a storeman but, if that could not be managed, an outsider could "switch" stores quite easily, provided that he knew roughly what would be on the invoices each time; observation might suffice. Orkney, although a delightfully different spot for a brief summer holiday and of course "home" to its inhabitants, produced in men condemned to serve there for a term of years with no known end, a dull lethargy known vulgarly as "Orkneyitis." Guard duty, all too often, was little more than a farce. Indeed, on an exercise, "B" Company of 2nd Gordons marched undetected from Rackwick on the west of Hoy to within one hundred yards of a battery then covering the Graemsay blockships. The attack, signaled by a smoke bomb from a two-inch mortar fired direct into the battery position, went in in full daylight, the assault platoons reaching the guns before the gunners had even stumbled out of their huts.

Similarly, if it was necessary to land the considerable

amount of high explosive required, in default of obtaining
it from local sources, then the operation, though not without melodrama, was virtually without risk. On a sparsely
populated island like Hoy there was a selection of suitable
spots. Indeed, the small number of inhabitants would present the first, and by far the most serious, obstacle to any
sabotage operation; the initial infiltration of the spy would
be immensely tricky—the newcomer would stick out like a
sore thumb.

Walter Schellenberg, in his memoirs, stated that a German spy was infiltrated into the Orkneys in the 1920s. If it
was done at all, that was when it was done. It was in 1924
that E. F. Cox, of the ship salvage firm of Cox & Danks,
decided to buy the German High Seas Fleet, lift the sev-
enty-two ships involved, and break them up for scrap. This
immense task took years and involved the arrival in Orkney of a number of outside workers, besides the divers.
Most lived in a camp, but some settled in with the crofters,
all within easy reach of the headquarters, which was—at
Lyness. The fanciful "Watchmaker Spy of Kirkwall" stories
have all ignored the fact that, although Kirkwall is the
capital of Orkney, it is remote from the naval base, which is
—at Lyness. Probably the authors did not know that; they
just jumped to conclusions.

At Thurso, while some of the survivors intensively discussed what had sunk their ship, a good many did not
bother their heads about it; they went to the pictures. Sergeant Booth did. The main feature was, "The Submarine
Menace."

But, with all this buzz of heated talk going on, there arrived, in force, in Thurso—the press. All survivors were
forthwith given strict security warnings—"under no circumstances communicate with the press." The number of
explosions was secret, the *Pegasus* was secret, the *Voltaire*

was secret—none of this was to be communicated even to relatives. The result was that the pressmen spent their time in pubs, plying survivors with drink, and getting in return very remarkable experiences of personal survival. In consequence, none of the main facts ever leaked out. It was years before it began to dawn on suspicious German naval writers that the *Repulse* had not been there at the material time—Prien had said so, therefore it was so—and as late as 1958 the self-appointed historian of the U-boats, Wolfgang Frank, could conjecture that the first torpedo had struck either the *Pegasus,* the *Royal Oak,* or the *Iron Duke!*

Late on Thursday, October 19th, the buzz went round that the leave train was raising steam. Sergeant Parham was still down on the list of witnesses from whom a detailed statement was required; at the last moment he was told to get on, they had enough evidence already. Eventually, only Captain Benn and Commander Nichols were left behind, to help with the Court of Enquiry. Lieutenant Benton had to give up a deerstalk, which had been arranged by Lady Sinclair—the officers were accommodated at the Air Minister's residence, and this was the least of the hospitality offered them.

The leave train looked as if it were peopled by brigands —there was hardly a complete uniform there. Overcoats, already on order from Rosyth, arrived just before the train started. Men walked down the carriages, dishing them out. "How many in here? Four? Right, here you are!" And four overcoats sailed in, any size.

Farley huddled himself up in his overcoat and, after a stop at Stirling for coffee and cocoa from the W.V.S., tried to go to sleep. A reporter, Farley thought he was from *The Daily Herald,* was playing cards with the other men in the compartment. The train gathered speed—then shuddered to a stop with a violent crash. With reflexes now much

sharpened, the other survivors were through the window in
a flash, followed by the reporter. Farley came out from under his overcoat in the corner, to see that the luggage rack
had fallen, one end of the seat had collapsed, and, where
the carriage door had been, a raw truck load of pig iron
was staring him in the face. The reporter was traveling fast
towards the nearest telephone, shouting out words that
sounded like, "Boy, oh, boy, what a scoop!" and pursued by
lieutenant commanders intent on stopping any more alarm-
ist stories getting out.

They had been rammed, at slow speed, by a freight
train; it just happened that Farley's compartment actually
took the impact. After a delay, they got in motion again,
reaching Glasgow about nine A.M. on the Friday. A sau-
sage-and-mash breakfast had been prepared at a restaurant
opposite the station; as they marched across the road in
their motley attire, a harsh chorus of jeers, boos and cat-
calls met them from a crowd which was beginning to
gather. As they marched back, after the meal, the same
crowd burst into a roar of cheering. Word had spread that
they were *Royal Oak* survivors, not German prisoners.

From Euston they were taken across to Waterloo. When
the train ran through Portsmouth town station, on the last
mile of the seven hundred, they were flat out—"worn to a
frazzle, it was like a ghost train." It went straight through
to Unicorn sidings in the dockyard, from where they were
taken to the Royal Naval Barracks—everything had been
prepared for them; and those who lived locally could go
home for what remained of the night, if they wanted. As
Batterbury stepped out of the gates for the first time into a
blacked-out Portsmouth, somebody rushed at him from the
unexpected darkness and flung her arms round his neck;
after a moment, he realized that it was his fiancée. Farley
had a different reception. He was stopped by a newsreel

cameraman who fitted him up with a wife and two kids for a touching reunion. He only had one child at the time, and the wife wasn't his either, but it looked all right.

The Marines were taken to Eastney Barracks, three officers and forty men. There were more than eighty missing faces. Any of the survivors who lived locally would be taken home by truck, provided they reported at the barracks next morning. "Local" really meant Eastney and, at the most, Southsea. But they went further and further through the city, the driver stretching things more and more. He dropped the last man off at Portchester, miles outside Portsmouth. "Where do you live, chum?" he asked Saltmarsh, who hadn't the heart to say it was Gosport, seven miles further on. He compromised on Fareham, and walked home five miles through the night.

Many of the wounded, however, were still many months from home. The worst cases, who were kept at Invergordon, still could not sleep at night; so they talked or sang in snatches to each other. The hospital was new, they were its first patients; some of the orderlies were miners. Fossey still has a card autographed by a doctor, Surgeon Lieutenant Bryan C. Murless, R.N.V.R., Sister Mary A. Montgomery, and nurses Molly Davidson and Elizabeth Ferguson. What each man feared was permanent disfigurement; they were afraid of what they would see when the bandages round their heads came off. For some there was the additional fear that their limbs would be permanently crippled. Stoker Tate and Leading Seaman Instance were the two most serious cases out of the fifteen who were kept there; after a few days, Tate died.

Changing the bandages was agony, cries of "brutal bitch" rang round the ward whenever it was done (although, privately, they all thought the staff were magnificent). The doctor decided that the pain was too much for already weakened men to suffer—there was fuel oil in the burns—and he introduced a system of wetting the bandages in a large tray, which got them off with much less discomfort. Instance was the most difficult case, because he required an operation to replace the flesh burned off his hands—the blazing cordite had attacked the raised portions more than anything else. After six weeks, a skin graft was made to his right hand, which was then strapped up on a rest resembling a miniature crane. It had to be left untouched for a week but, as the smell became worse, Instance swiveled it away from under his nose. The patient in the next bed, much put out, pushed it back.

At length, when the seven days had passed Sister Montgomery placed screens round him before starting to take off the bandages; other curious burn cases began to crowd round the screens, peering over the top. But as the layers of bandage came off, the odor became more and more distinct and the number of heads looking over the screens became fewer and fewer. After a while, there was none; finally, the Sister herself could stand it no longer and fled for a nip of brandy. When the hand was bared at last, it was just a horrible mass of pus. Instance tried to joke: "Let me have a nip, too—I've had to live with this thing." At that point the doctor judged that Instance's morale was low—"so it was," said Instance—and sent for his wife to come up and join him. When she arrived, it was too late—the pus had gone and the hand was "clean as a whistle."

On November 20th Kerr, Dommett, Campbell, Thatcher, Hancock, Hearn and Bond were discharged. They took the train for Euston, still in their makeshift clothes, with not a shred of naval uniform among them. Kerr's burns had cleared up, except for his ears, which still looked a bit like "the crackling off roasted pork," and his hair, which was burned away at the front and on top. As they passed through the barrier at Euston, they heard two soldiers call out, "We're looking for seven sailors who're supposed to be on this train."

Kerr spun round. "That's us!"

The soldiers stood a moment, gazing. "Blimey!" said one, "where's Snow White?"

With two weeks to Christmas, Instance was alone in the ward. On Christmas Eve, he traveled south with his wife, unable to wear uniform and with his hands protected by special gloves. In the train were a number of servicemen and to make conversation one of them turned to Instance with, "Been touring the Highlands?" Instance told him. At a halt on the long journey, he badly wanted a cup of tea, but there was a terrific crowd at the canteen, so that neither he nor his wife stood a chance of getting one. At length, a sergeant appeared—holding two cups of tea. He was followed by a Marine—with two cups of tea. Bringing up the rear was a sailor—with two cups of tea. The same idea having occurred to all three independently, the cups of tea were at last laid in rows on the floor of the carriage.

Instance, in his recovery, showed the same inflexible determination which had enabled him to survive; although his right hand never did regain its full use, with the aid of one doctor, he got round the others, remained in the Navy and is today a lieutenant. For some time afterwards he was not happy in ships, particularly at night, and, because his escape had been due to knowing the *Royal Sovereign* class inside out, he made it his business to be able to walk round the ship with his eyes shut. Bendell, who had been trapped below, took his own lesson to heart and slept on deck as much as he could, wearing a lanyard, a knife and a whistle.

Other survivors of the *Royal Oak* did not survive the war. Cleverley saw Chief Stoker W. H. Aplin during the Norwegian campaign (they lived in the same road and knew each other well); they had a few hours talk before Aplin left in the destroyer *Acasta* for home; on the way he met the *Scharnhorst* and *Gneisnau.*

Boy Trewinnard was drafted to the armed merchant cruiser *Vandyke,* a sister ship of the *Voltaire;* in her was another *Royal Oak* survivor, Sick Berth Petty Officer William Brigden. The *Vandyke* also met her end in the Norwegian campaign. Trewinnard was taken prisoner and spent five years in German P.O.W. camps, until he was freed by a Russian force led by a motorcycle and sidecar. Although he can now recall little of the *Royal Oak,* he can vividly remember the amazing spectacle of the Red Army advance, a mass of horses, carts, and men on foot mixed up with brand-new Lend-Lease American trucks.

The Court of Enquiry cannot have found any fault with Captain Benn, for he was afterwards given another ship, the cruiser *Fiji;* curiously enough, half a dozen *Royal Oak* survivors, including Boxall, were among her crew when she sailed with the Dakar expedition and Lieutenant Benton was in another ship of the convoy. He was looking directly at the *Fiji,* when he saw a white water column leap up her side—she had been torpedoed.

Lawrence was in the destroyer *Worcester* when she had her stern blown off by an eleven-inch shell from the *Scharnhorst.* Wilson "ditched" once more, from a corvette; so did Blundell, from the *Ark Royal;* Leading Telegraphist Jones was in the cruiser *Birmingham* when she was either mined or torpedoed (it was never known which) off Benghazi. In fact, a good many, in one way or another, subsequently acquired substantial knowledge of marine explosions; and they were divided in their opinion. Some thought that a real torpedo felt nothing like what happened to the *Royal Oak;* others felt it was exactly the same sort of thing. The explanation was, of course, that it all depended on where you were in relation to the explosion.

By the end of the war Prien was dead, and so were Endrass and von Varendorff, his two executive officers, whose questioning might have helped to resolve the really remarkable discrepancies between what actually took place in Scapa Flow and what Prien said had happened. However, the log of U.47 was captured, along with almost all the files of the German Admiralty; this, far from clearing up the matter, increased the mystery. Prien's wartime statements and the autobiography attributed to him might have been passed off as propaganda, but this was an official document and what it revealed was a mixture of the untrue, the incredible and the impossible. On the one hand there were the survivors of the *Royal Oak* describing, as it were, a blizzard at the North Pole, and on the other hand the U-boat commander who was supposed to have sunk them talking about a Carnival in Venice. It was a fair deduction that they had not been to the same place.

13

"How I Sank the *Royal Oak*"

The official German version is contained in the log of U.47. This records that, having passed Duncansby Head—the northeastern tip of Scotland—the U-boat was in position off the Orkneys on Thursday, October 12th. After dark, she surfaced and closed the coast in order to fix her position exactly. The gale through which the *Royal Oak* had struggled during her patrol in the Fair Isle Channel was now abating, but the dark waters of the Pentland Firth were foam capped and the sky was blanketed by gray rain clouds. After the fixes had been taken, U.47 submerged and, at four A.M. on Friday the 13th, Prien ordered his crew to assemble in the forward mess. "Tomorrow we shall enter Scapa Flow," were his first words.

The crew had guessed that something unusual was afoot, but this was the first intimation of what their task was to be. There was silence, as they considered the implications. There had been two attempts during the first world war to penetrate the Scapa defenses—and both U-boats had been lost, one of them with all hands. They were all aware that death for a submariner comes usually as a claustrophobic affair in darkness—a brief, choking struggle inside a riven steel box under the crushing and appalling weight of many tons of water.

Having gained their attention, Prien went on to explain that this attack was to be carried out on the surface; if things went wrong, there was still a chance, and they were to prepare scuttling charges, in case the boat had to be destroyed. In the meantime, they were to keep quiet and to sleep, if possible. Their last hot meal would be in twelve hours time; after that, sandwiches only. They would be going into Scapa Flow.

U.47 was a medium-sized boat of five hundred tons, 213 feet long, with a surface speed of just over sixteen knots; she carried four twenty-one-inch torpedo tubes in the bow and another twenty-one-inch tube at the stern. She had been in commission for less than a year.

At four P.M. on Friday, October 13th, her crew of some thirty-five men had their last hot meal before the attack and then placed two torpedoes ready for rapid re-loading in the bow. All torpedoes carried on this operation were of the G7e type; powered by electric motors, they were slow-running and lacked the penetration of the faster G7a torpedo. Their advantage was that they left no telltale "track" on the surface. As they would be fired in comparatively shallow water at deep-draught ships, the new magnetic fuses, which would explode a torpedo under the bottom of a ship, were not used; the old-fashioned but reliable impact fuses were fitted. No very great penetration could be expected; the explosions would be at the side of the ship, not under it or in it.

At 7:15 P.M., U.47 surfaced and began to move in towards the coast. The gale had now almost blown itself out and there was only a light wind from the north-northeast; steadily, it was pushing aside a bank of clouds. As it did so, the clouds themselves began to glow, as if concealing a gigantic bonfire, until the entire northern horizon was sending up flickering, tremulous shafts of bluish light—the "Merry Dancers" of the northern latitudes. Prien stared in astonishment at the display—in astonishment and consternation. The period of the new moon, when the northern night would normally be pitch dark, had deliberately been chosen for this enterprise. No one had thought of the aurora borealis.

The northern lights are rarely seen two nights in succession and if Prien waited for another twenty-four hours, he would probably be able to attack under cover of darkness. But his crew were now keyed up to make the attack; the long hours of waiting might take the keen edge off their enthusiasm. Prien decided that it was now, or never; and U.47 kept on for Rose Ness, the headland guarding the entrance to Holm Sound.

Almost at once, there was another alarm. Whipping his night glasses up to his eyes, Prien studied a dim object ahead; it was hard to make out, but it appeared to be a ship. Instantly, he ordered "diving stations" and took the boat down to periscope depth; but on neither of his periscopes could he now see anything at all. The dim shadow, fishing vessel or neutral ship, or whatever it was, had disappeared; or else it had never been there; or the northern lights were playing tricks with the periscopes.

When Prien judged it was safe to surface again, the time was 11:31 P.M. The northern lights were brighter than ever. The visibility was so exceptionally good that, when U.47 rounded Rose Ness and Prien saw a blockship ahead of him, he thought that he must be in Kirk Sound. In fact, Kirk Sound was still hidden by the headland. What he was looking at was the blockship in Skerry Sound, nearly one and a half miles away. As Kirk Sound came slowly into view, Prien realized his mistake and, almost simultaneously, his navigator corrected him. Prien sharply altered course to starboard, to make for Kirk Sound.

"*It is a very eerie sight,*" he noted for the log. "*On land everything is dark, high in the sky are the flickering northern lights, so that the bay, surrounded by highish mountains, is directly lit from above. The blockships lie in the Sound, ghostly as the wings of a theater.*"

The tidal stream, flowing into Scapa, bore the U-boat at great speed down upon the blockships. A two-masted schooner loomed ahead; Prien passed her with only a few yards to spare. Then the current swung the submarine's bow wildly to starboard. Engines going ahead, she was nevertheless carried sideways down upon the next blockship, a half-sunken steamer. In an effort to bring his boat into line, Prien stopped the port engine and, the starboard engine at slow ahead, gave the order to put the helm over hard to port. The U-boat touched the ground, her stern grated along the blockship's cable, then she was free.

Prien was in Scapa Flow, unseen. So narrow was the channel behind him, that he himself saw a cyclist pedaling along the coastal road on the northern side, apparently some late bird going home. The time now was twenty-seven minutes after midnight—it was Black Saturday. "*It is disgustingly light,*" he noted. "*The whole bay is lit up.*"

Prien turned the boat slowly to port and steered for the main fleet anchorage, where the battleships, battle cruisers and aircraft carriers would be lying. The scuttling of the German High Seas Fleet would finally be avenged in the very place in which it had occurred. But no masts and funnels loomed up against the sky. Prien went further in, until he could plainly see the bar boats guarding the boom in Hoxa Sound, until it seemed that in a minute or two they must surely see him. There was no sign of the big ships; he was certain of it, he could see for miles. The Home Fleet must have sailed.

One chance only remained—the cluster of ships in the northeast corner of the Flow, off Kirkwall. So Prien made a 180-degree turn and went back the way he had come, until, at a distance of over a mile, he could make out the dim loom of the cliffs ahead; then, keeping the coast in view on the starboard side, he steered north towards Scapa pier. And here, at five minutes to one in the morning, he saw his prey.

Two battleships lay ahead, broadside on to him, their bows pointed towards the nearest land—the cliffs which lay on the U-boat's starboard side. Nearer the shore, destroyers were moored. A tanker was visible, but no cruisers.

Prien chose the capital ships as his target, and he intended to get them both with the same salvo—a "fan" of four torpedoes from the bow. As the targets were deep-draught ships, he ordered the torpedoes to be set to run at 7.5 meters. At that depth, they would strike well below the armor belt.

At two minutes before one o'clock in the morning, U.47 fired her first salvo, with a few seconds interval between each torpedo, so that the helmsman could swing the bow around slightly and so achieve the "fan" or "spread." But in one tube there was a misfire, so that only three torpedoes left the bow and began their run towards the silent ships. Two had been aimed at the nearest ship—from her single funnel, apparently a battleship of the *Royal Sovereign* class —and one torpedo at the ship further away, which—judging by her two funnels—was the battle cruiser *Repulse*.

There was a deadly wait, as the seconds were counted off. "*After a good three and a half minutes,*" noted Prien, "*a torpedo detonates on the northern ship; of the other two nothing is to be seen.*"

The northern ship, the *Repulse*, had apparently been hit; but the expected alarm did not occur—the anchorage lay still and silent. And U.47 had one more sting left—the one in her tail. She turned slowly to starboard, coming closer to the cliffs, until eventually her stern torpedo tube pointed at the *Royal Sovereign* class battleship. Again the order to fire was given; and again the long seconds were counted off, as the torpedo ran towards the gigantic, stationary target. Nothing happened. The fourth torpedo had missed. Either it had been wrongly set for depth or the aim had been faulty, perhaps not enough allowance had been made for tidal drift. There was nothing to show, for the whole daring operation, except one hit on the battle cruiser which, Prien thought, was now badly down by the bow.

Down below, as U.47 headed for Kirk Sound once more, men were busily engaged in re-loading the bow tubes. There was still no alarm and there was a chance, just a chance, that the re-loading would be completed in time to make another attack. After covering more than a mile of the distance towards the entrance, Prien made his decision. U.47 turned to starboard through 180 degrees and headed back towards the "big fellows." The die was cast.

At 1:22 A.M., Prien was once again in an attacking position, two miles south of the two big ships. This time he would make certain of the *Royal Sovereign* class battleship —she was the easiest target, the one nearest to him. Three torpedoes left the bow, at intervals of a few seconds, as the helmsman put the wheel over, and for three minutes Prien waited, tense with apprehension.

Then the battleship seemed to erupt before his eyes, vanishing in a vast uprush of water. A few seconds after the explosion, a sound like a clap of thunder burst over Scapa Flow. A drumfire of explosions followed, fairly splitting the night. The sky paled and vanished altogether in the savage glow of the explosion flashes and the flames which followed them. Giant black shadows—jagged fragments of the battleship's masts and funnel—soared upwards, silhouetted by the red blaze of light, and fell in leaping gouts of water into the Flow. Then there was nothing there at all—the battleship had gone, torn to pieces by the explosion of her own magazines and shell rooms within a matter of only two or three seconds.

The British may have been sleeping, before this; they were awake now! *"The harbor springs to life,"* noted Prien. *"Destroyers are lit up, signaling starts on every side, and on land two hundred meters away from me cars roar along the roads."*

If Prien had displayed inventiveness in his version so far, it was as nothing compared to the creative imagination he would now display. Directly opposite U.47, a car stopped abruptly; then Prien saw its headlights flashing as it turned right around and finally accelerated away down the road to Scapa pier and Kirkwall. It had seen the U-boat, it must have; nothing else could account for its actions. Now, brilliantly lit up by the dangerous radiance of the northern lights, the whole vast anchorage a hive of ships stirring into motion against them, the Germans' chances of escape were slim. They had sunk a battleship, they had apparently damaged a battle cruiser, in spite of the torpedo failures. It was not the overwhelming success Dönitz had hoped for, but they would have to be content with it. Searchlights—white, shifting fingers—were sending their glare across the dark water; lights were flashing, zigzagging here and there; destroyers and submarine-chasers were hunting the U-boat.

Prien turned for Holm Sound and raced away at sixteen knots on the surface, both engines full ahead, heedless of the white wake he was leaving behind him. It must have been seen, for a destroyer stood away from the welter of wildly searching lights in the Flow and came tearing after them. Capable of more than twice the speed of the U-boat, she was overtaking rapidly.

And now, as they came into Holm Sound, the U-boat met the full force of the tide, pressing at ten knots through the narrow channel into the Flow. She was held motionless by that enormous torrent of water, the spray foaming past her steel sides. She was held like a butterfly pinned to a board, while the destroyer raced up from astern.

At first, all Prien could see of it was its masthead light, bearing down on them; but gradually, the sharp silhouette appeared—without doubt, it was a destroyer. At any moment it would open fire at its helpless target.

Then, suddenly, inexplicably, the shape of the destroyer's silhouette began to alter; it became longer, a gap appeared between mast and funnel, and the gap was lengthening. Their enemy was turning away. In the maelstrom of tossing water, it could not have seen their wake.

And then, somehow, the U-boat was through into the main channel of the Sound, both engines hammering away at full ahead now, and the electric motors coupled up as well, to give the last ounce of speed. Leaving a high wash behind, tossed thankfully astern, U.47 twisted and turned among the blockships. A mole loomed up ahead. The helm went hard over, then centered—and she was free! Behind her, as she slipped into the open sea, came the repeated thunder of depth charges as the destroyers and sub-chasers, too late, scored the anchorage with high explosives.

"0215," noted Prien. "*Set southeast course for base. I still have five torpedoes for possible attacks on merchantmen.*"

At 0630, just before first light, it was time to submerge, but Prien could not resist looking back at the scene of his great triumph. *"The glow from Scapa is still visible for a long time. Apparently they are still dropping depth charges."*

On the morning of October 17th, U.47 entered Wilhelmshaven, to meet the reception due to heroes. That afternoon, some of the crew were flown to Kiel and some to Berlin. Prien told his story to Dönitz, *"Royal Oak blew up within a few seconds—observed great anti-U-boat activity (with depth charges) in Scapa Flow—was greatly bothered by brilliance of northern lights."* Breathlessly, the details came out. He told his story to the press, he told his story to the world on radio, soon afterwards he wrote his "autobiography"—and, after the war, his log was among the enemy documents captured by the Allies. These are the sources, official and semiofficial, from which this account of the sinking of the *Royal Oak* and the damaging of the *Repulse*, as seen by Prien, has been reconstructed.

Prien himself did not survive the war, nor did his three watchkeeping officers in U.47; and that is a pity, because the men who really were in Scapa Flow on the night of October 13-14, 1939, contradict Prien's story in almost all its main particulars. The present author interviewed, or corresponded with, fifty-four of them, forty-six being survivors of the *Royal Oak*.

Prien complained about the brilliance of the night; the survivors of the *Royal Oak*, and Skipper Gatt, who had to pick them up, complained about the darkness, which made the work of rescue so difficult. "Pitch black," "the dark night," are phrases which crop up in accounts they wrote at the time. Prien was dismayed by the spectacle of the northern lights; the survivors do not remember such a spectacle—"a dark but starlit night" sums up their general recollection. Prien, under extreme tension, would have believed himself to have been more conspicuous than he really was, but this is not sufficient to explain such a discrepancy.

Prien claimed to have damaged the *Repulse* so badly that her bow sank "deep into the water"; in fact, he did not hit her at all. She wasn't there. German apologists have suggested that he might have hit the *Iron Duke* instead; this battleship had two funnels and might have been mistaken for the *Repulse*. The *Iron Duke* was not hit—and as she was ten miles away, that is not surprising. The British official historian suggests that Prien mistook the *Pegasus* for the *Repulse*, but he did not, because he could not have seen the *Pegasus*—she was lying to the northwest of the *Royal Oak* in a position in which it was hard to see the camouflaged bulk of the battleship *Nelson* in broad daylight, because of the cliffs behind. She could not have been mistaken for the *Repulse* anyway, because she was a weird-looking ship with a single spindly funnel aft and was not only much smaller than the battle cruiser, but very much further away than in Prien's description. The laws of perspective can make a large ship, far away, seem like a small ship quite near; but the facts, in this case, are the opposite—the 366-foot, 6,900-ton *Pegasus*, nearly two miles from the *Royal Oak*, being mistaken for the eight-hundred-foot long, 32,000-ton *Repulse*, lying just behind the *Royal Oak*. This would be rather like mistaking a baby down at the end of the garden path for a hulking wrestler standing on the doorstep. In any case, the *Pegasus* was not hit.

What other ship might Prien have confused with the *Repulse?* The cruel answer is that the *Royal Oak* and the *Pegasus* were the only ships that night in the northeast corner of the Flow. Not only was there no *Repulse,* but there were no destroyers either, nor was there a tanker. *Royal Oak* and *Pegasus* were alone—and widely separated. And now we come to the most remarkable discrepancy of all.

Prien speaks all the time of the "southern ship" (*Royal Oak*) and the "northern ship" (*Repulse*); the careful chart which accompanies the log remorselessly bears out this incredible mistake. There are the two "big fellows" lying to the north of Prien, their starboard sides open to him and their bows pointed at the nearest land—that is to say, east. Certainly there were two ships there, the big *Royal Oak* and the small *Pegasus,* two miles to the west of the *Royal Oak.* What Prien was looking at, if he was there at all, was not a southern ship and a northern ship, but an eastern ship and a western ship. And, furthermore, if he was in the position he says he was, then their starboard sides were not presented to him—he was looking at their sterns. For the *Royal Oak* and the *Pegasus* were not headed east, as Prien says; they were headed *north.* In particular, the bow of the *Royal Oak* was not pointed at the nearest land, her starboard side was *parallel* to it. The witnesses say so; the Tide Tables, which show the tide going out, indicate it; and the divers who went down to the wreck confirm it. The *Royal Oak's* bow was headed north towards Kirkwall. From his southerly position, it would have been absolutely impossible for Prien to have torpedoed her in her starboard side.

In order to do that, he would have to have crept into that narrow half-mile stretch of water between the *Royal Oak* and the shore and fire almost due west instead of due north, as he says. And in order to do that, the whole attack plan of the U-boat, as shown in detail on the chart, must be moved very nearly through a right angle. When this is done, a startling fact becomes clear. The distance from the *Royal Oak* to land was half a mile; Prien says (and his chart confirms) that U.47's firing positions were two miles from the starboard side of the battleship; therefore, Prien must have made both his attacks from a position nearly one and a half miles *inland*.

Even allowing for Prien's undoubted professional skill, to which Mr. Churchill has duly paid tribute, this strains credulity.

Nor is it possible to believe that this was an honest mistake, some error of navigation perhaps. It involves mistaking west and north; it involves nearly a ninety degree error in the heading of the U-boat herself, when both compass and chart (for the line of the cliffs would have been visible) make an error of more than a few degrees impossible, even for an amateur. We are not here dealing with a submerged attack, possibly in a rough sea, the target seen momentarily through a spray-drenched periscope with its restricted and indifferent view. Prien was on the surface, Prien had plenty of time, Prien was not being shot at, and the visibility, said Prien, was almost too good. Additionally, he had a navigating officer. And, most important of all, there is no motive which could conceivably have led him to make a knowingly false statement on this point. Obviously, Prien, if he was there, had no idea what ships were in the northeast corner of the Flow, no idea of their heading, no idea of his own heading, and no idea where he was. And his officers, one of whom actually came up on deck, must have been similarly clueless. This, too, strains credulity. However did they manage to find their way back to Germany at all—or arrive at Scapa Flow in the first place?

Prien reported to Dönitz that his second salvo sank the *Royal Oak* "in a few seconds" and, in his autobiography, said that a shell room must have blown up. But the *Royal*

Oak, unlike the *Vanguard,* did not blow up and did not sink within seconds. A cordite magazine "vented" but did not explode; the ship listed, turned slowly over, and was upside down about seven or nine minutes later. *"We found no trace whatever of any magazine explosion,"* reported Captain W. R. Fell, R.N., who commanded the 1951 diving survey of the *Royal Oak.* The only magazine found by the divers to be wrecked, possibly by explosion, contained small-arms ammunition—.303 rifle and machine-gun cartridges. The "explosion," if it took place, could hardly be compared to that of 208 fifteen-inch shells, which anyway would have set off the other three fifteen-inch shell rooms.

Prien stated that this (totally fictitious) detonation instantly woke up the whole of Scapa Flow. *"The harbor springs to life. Destroyers are lit up, signaling starts on every side, and on land 200 meters away from me cars roar along the roads,"* is his dramatic version of the scene. Scapa Flow did *not* spring to life; like the nearest ship, the *Pegasus,* it remained dark and silent. The only moving thing was the drifter *Daisy II,* and as she had a rope wrapped around her screw, she was not moving very fast; she was burning two dim lights—and that was all the light there was. There were, in short, no searchlights, no signaling, no destroyers, lit up or otherwise, and, it must be added, no car on that road "200 meters away," because, in fact, there was no road there. The nearest road was nearly *three-quarters of a mile inland.*

Nor was there any depth charging. Prien described in his "autobiography" the destroyer which pursued him into Holm Sound at, presumably, thirty-six knots. The only small vessel within miles was the crippled drifter, searching slowly for survivors in the immediate area of the sinking. And, not only was she three miles away, she was actu-

ally out of sight behind Skaildaquoy Point. Artistically,
the "destroyer" is a thrilling climax to the tale; factually,
neither she nor her depth charges existed. Nor, for that
matter, did the ten-knot current which held U.47 motionless, as she struggled to escape.

The tide was *not* coming in at ten knots; it was actually
going *out*. The Tide Tables make that clear, particularly
when combined with the evidence of local witnesses. High
tide in Kirk Sound on the night of Friday, October 13th,
was at about ten P.M. As there was no wind to delay it or
to push it on, the beginning of the ebb tide would have
been at about midnight. Between the hours of 1:30 A.M.
and 2:15 A.M. on Saturday, when Prien was making his escape, the tide would have been going out fairly strongly.
He would have had the tide with him, but what he de-
scribes is a desperate struggle against a tide race pouring
into Scapa Flow. The next high tide was not in fact due
until 10:20 on Saturday morning.

That Prien was unscrupulous with regard to what he entered in the log, is made clear by a later exploit. Having
dealt with the *Royal Oak* and the *Repulse* in October, he
sank the big cruiser *Norfolk* in November. To the crew of
the *Norfolk*, it made not the slightest difference—they returned undamaged to harbor, unaware even that Prien
had attacked them. An explosion hundreds of yards astern,
they attributed to a stray bomb dropped from above the
clouds; actually it was a torpedo from U.47 which had exploded on hitting the wake of the cruiser. Prien hurried
back home with a report, full of circumstantial detail, of
the explosion damage he had plainly seen on the cruiser's
upper deck; and in consequence of being unable to find her
afterwards, he claimed that she must have sunk.

It must be conceded that this attack was made, sub-

merged, in a gale; even so, Dönitz, who probably knew his
Prien, dryly commented: "From the serviceman's point of
*view such inaccuracies and exaggerations are unde-
sirable.*"

But it is true also that Prien was very willing to let himself be used by the German Propaganda Service and for
this reason was disliked by some of the other U-boat "aces,"
who felt that this was degrading to the Navy as a whole, as
well as to the individual concerned. *"You don't write your
own story,"* admitted one of them. *"They write it for you
—and make you look a bloody fool."* It was Prien's "autobiography" he was probably thinking of, because he himself steadfastly refused to have anything to do with Dr.
Goebbels.

On the other hand, some of the most glaring errors in
Prien's story cannot be accounted for in any way other
than by the supposition that he was not there. And if he
was not there, and if the *Royal Oak* was in fact sunk by
sabotage, then Goebbels, looking for a likely man to carry
off a masquerade suggested by the British Admiralty's
early admission of her loss, "believed by U-boat action,"
need hardly have looked further than Prien, particularly
as the deception would serve a patriotic purpose.

But that deception, at the beginning of the war, would
have had to be maintained right through the war and indeed afterwards. What precedents are there for this? To
the author's knowledge, one only—the log of U.30 which,
contrary to orders, sank the liner *Athenia* in September,
1939. Goebbels broadcast a denial and was not prepared
to retract, therefore the incriminating page of the log was
removed and another page substituted, the captain and
crew of U.30 being sworn to a secrecy which they faithfully maintained. The log was faked, not to keep the news
from the world, but to keep it quiet actually within the

German Admiralty; there was no thought then of possible defeat, of foreigners going through the records. But go through these records they eventually did, searching on the highest orders for possible war criminals. In these circumstances, with the spotlight very much on the *Athenia* sinking, the truth at last came out. But the *Royal Oak* operation was an act of war, not an atrocity, and there was no such pressure in her case.

In short, fabrications of this order require government action and a strong motive; the same requirements generally hold good if the fabrication is to be exposed.

But the British also had upheld Prien's story—and what motive could they have? At the time, they had a very strong motive indeed—the widespread depression at the Scapa base generally, and not merely confined to survivors, at the thought of unseen enemy agents who might strike again at any time. The announcement that the *Royal Oak* had definitely been sunk by a U-boat did in fact do a great deal for morale, although only about half the survivors were convinced. The rest believe to this day that it was not a U-boat. It is not Prien's log, nor his autobiography, which convinces them that his exploit is fictitious—most of them have read neither the one nor the other. Mainly, their contempt for the story is based on the fact that his "torpedoes" exploded, in every case, in the vicinity of a storeroom into which stores had been put a few hours previously; and that there were *no* explosions anywhere else. They would also like to know why a U-boat captain should choose to attack from the cramped and difficult position on the starboard side, when, on the port side, he had the whole of Scapa Flow in which to maneuver. Those who knew of the secrecy in which the diving survey was being conducted, were also made suspicious by this, as, indeed, was the present author when he found that the 1939 survey was *still*

secret and that no permission could be had to look at a
scale model of the wreck, showing position and areas of
damage, the existence—and even the location—of which
he was able to establish. This, the details of the damage,
taken together with a constructor's plan of the ship, would
have established beyond all doubt whether the explosions
had been internal or external.

One clue only, when followed up, yielded a return. This
was a report from a senior officer that he had been shown
recovered parts of two of the torpedoes which had sunk
the *Royal Oak*. The Admiralty eventually sent two files of
reports, dated December, 1939 and January, 1940. Subject: torpedo parts found in Scapa Flow in vicinity of
Royal Oak wreck.

As the battleship had carried four twenty-one-inch torpedo tubes in the bow, and part of her stem and keel had
been blown away, the finding of torpedo parts proved
nothing; they had to be German torpedoes. The reports,
very detailed and obviously genuine, said that they were;
indeed, even a German nameplate had been recovered.
Technically, the information tallied almost exactly with
the information available from the German side—with one
exception. The torpedoes had been fired, concluded the
British reports, from a range that was almost certainly less
than one mile. And that fitted the facts, even if it did not
agree with Prien's log.

If these reports are accepted at face value, it follows that
Prien was in Scapa Flow after all, but for reasons unknown
chose to give an almost totally false account of how he
sank the *Royal Oak*. It could be conjectured that some of
his fictitious descriptive matter, such as the good visibility,
the explosion of the battleship's magazines, and the subse-
quent stirring up of the anchorage, would provide an ex-
cuse for his speedy retirement. He reported leaving the

base of the British Home Fleet with five torpedoes un-
expended, an action which might be human, but was
hardly heroic. For these three pieces of fiction he had
therefore a plainly possible motive; but only mental
acrobatics of the highest order could explain the error in
the headings and the contradiction of the Tide Tables.

The British Admiralty, as previously noted, hate telling
lies, although in wartime, to avoid giving away vital information, it is sometimes very hard not to. They probably
believe, understandably, that it is not a good thing to get
a reputation for lack of veracity; indeed, to find a parallel
case to the *Royal Oak* one would have to go back several
centuries to a similarly named ship, the *Royal George*,
which sank in peculiar circumstances in the British main
fleet anchorage at Spithead, off Portsmouth, in 1782. More
than eight hundred men were lost and nearly four hundred
saved, almost exactly as in the *Royal Oak*. The Admiralty
did not tell lies about her—they merely kept the court-
martial very quiet and firmly blocked all efforts to raise the
wreck, while giving the appearance of being eager to see it
come up. In consequence, a most extraordinary story got
abroad, was written up in memorable verse by a considerable poet, and is faithfully believed in England today, even
in Portsmouth.

The *Royal George* had been unfortunately capsized, it
was said, while heeled for below the waterline repairs, by a
"land breeze." To anyone in possession of the facts, it was
a quite inadequate explanation; but there is now no need
to delve the mystery—the court-martial proceedings can
be examined any day in the Public Record Office in Lon-
don. The court decided that the frame of the ship had
been rotten and that the bottom, quite literally, had fallen
out of her. At the time—there was a war on—this reve-
lation would have been political dynamite; hence the se-

crecy. Hence also why no one in authority contradicted the sea-happy poet, William Cowper.

The case of the *Royal Oak* poses a mystery which is not likely to be finally cleared up in our time, and it has already fathered a number of myths which promise to outdo even Cowper's stirring poem, "Toll for the Brave." Prien himself is already a myth; it is whispered now that he did not die at sea—sunk in U.47 by H.M.S. *Wolverine*—but perished in a concentration camp, or in a penal battalion on the Russian front, for mutiny, or as a prisoner of war in the United States.

And a fresh character has come to join him—the fabulous "Watchmaker of Kirkwall," a child's version of a spy who is said to have more or less led Prien by the hand into Scapa Flow. This story appeared first as an unsigned article on a Berlin newspaper in December, 1947, and has since been widely repeated. There is a splendid scene, in the original version of this story, in which the U-boat (called the BO-6) is navigated through the Flow by the old Swiss watchmaker (really a German naval officer in disguise). They pass, as if in review, down the lines of the entire British Home Fleet, assembled for inspection. But the old watchmaker will have none of them, until at length he comes to the last ship in the line (laid down, 1914). "That one," he says, "the *Royal Oak*—pride of the British Navy!"

Since the publication, in 1948, of Prien's log, the "Watchmaker" has lost some of his more diverting details, following a surgical operation which has joined his fabulous story to the equally fabulous tale told by Prien. From all the signs, the resulting concoction is due for a very long run. It seems almost a shame to point out that, internal evidence apart, the number of German naval officers posing in Kirkwall as old Swiss watchmakers must of necessity be strictly limited, and that no one in Kirk-wall—let alone Mr. W. Hourston, the leading jeweler and watchmaker in the town—has ever heard of Alfred Oertel, the "Watchmaker of Kirkwell."

The *Royal Oak* lies now on her starboard side, slowly sinking into the sandy bottom of Scapa Flow and turning over. Her fifteen-inch guns have been forced upwards, by the sand, to full elevation and her masts and funnel are buckling upwards. On her port side, which is turned now towards the silvery light filtering down from the surface, seaweed is growing in profusion; shell and anemone cake her keel and those parts of her upper decks on which the light can fall. Where the hull narrows at the bow, it is clear of the sand and, in 1951 at least, a diver could walk underneath.

In the Paint Store area, that is, near the Inflammable Store, the stem and keel have been blown away; amidships, in the engine rooms, boiler rooms and Central Stores, there is a chaos of wreckage blurred to view by the silt stirred up by a diver's movements.

In December, 1957, the Admiralty invited bids for the salvage and scrapping of the wreck, but this brought a storm of protest from the relatives of the dead men who lie inside the shattered hull. "You would not go to a cemetery and dig up coffins," said one. "These sailors have no proper graves," said another, "they should be left in peace where they are." In face of these protests, the admiralty had to abandon the project. And now, in peace, they lie.

Acknowledgments

I must express my gratitude to the many people who gave freely of their time in order to help me reconstruct the events as precisely as possible. Thirty-three witnesses were interviewed at length; many others wrote for me long and detailed accounts. Others again went to great trouble to help track down "key" witnesses among the survivors.

For the contemporary narratives, which were especially valuable, I am deeply indebted to Mr. J. Kerr, who loaned me his scrapbook which contained not only his own very full account but the stories of twelve other survivors who were with him at the time in hospital; to the Headmaster of Ardvreck, for permission to quote from Midshipman Pirie's narrative, which was published in the December, 1939, issue of the school magazine; to Skipper Gatt for unearthing after much search a pamphlet, "Sea Samaritans," containing a re-print from *The Orcadian* of October 10, 1940, of his article on the rescue operations; and to Mr. R. Jones for letting me see a copy of *The Citizen*, of October 30, 1939, in which his own personal experiences were reported at length. Also to Commander R.A.V.

Gregory for the opportunity to look through some of his lecture notes on the subject, made shortly after. A number of survivors were able to supply photographs, most of which had in fact been taken by Sick Berth Attendant Bendell, who does not have a complete set, because his negatives are still in the wreck.

It was intended to contact at least ten per cent of the survivors in order to achieve a reasonable cross section of the ship's company; this was more than achieved, but there are nevertheless a few gaps, due to heavy casualties in particular messes. I have not attempted to fill these by hearsay because, although most of those stories which were related at second hand proved on further investigation to be basically true, there had been a certain blurring of detail; they had deteriorated with age, whereas first-hand experiences had been too vivid to forget.

I have to thank the following survivors of H.M.S. *Royal Oak* for their help in the reconstruction:

	Rank at the Time
Commander G. Affleck-Graves, R.N. (Retd.)	Flag-Lieutenant
Mr. W. G. T. Batterbury	Leading Supply Assistant
Sick Berth Chief Petty Officer R. G. Bendell, R.N.	Sick Berth Attendant
Major M. H. Benton, R.M. (Retd.)	Lieutenant, R.M.
Lieutenant T. W. Blundell, R.N. (Retd.)	Acting Petty Officer
Mr. G. H. Booth	Sergeant, R.M.
Surgeon Captain E. D. Caldwell, R.N.	Surgeon Lieutenant
Mr. H. P. Cleverley	Stoker

Rear Admiral J. R. Cundall, C.B.E., R.N. (Retd.)	Paymaster Commander
Mr. E. G. Dommett	Ordnance Artificer
Commander H. Duncan, D.S.C., R.N.	Lieutenant
Mr. A. J. Farley	Able Seaman
Mr. N. J. Finley	Supply Petty Officer
Mr. W. J. Fossey	Leading Signalman
Commander R. A. V. Gregory, R.N. (Retd.)	Lieutenant Commander
Mr. B. S. C. Hawes	Marine
Lieutenant H. J. Instance, R.N.	Leading Seaman
Mr. T. H. Jones	Leading Stoker
Mr. R. S. Jones	Leading Telegraphist
Major B. Keen, R.M. (Retd.)	Lieutenant, R.M.
Mr. J. R. Kerr	Petty Officer (Div. P.O.)
Mr. A. Lawrence, D.S.M. and Bar	Chief Stoker
Mr. J. McLaverty	Sergeant, R.M.
Commander E. G. S. Maclean, R.N. (Retd.)	Lieutenant Commander
Captain R. F. Nichols, R.N. (Retd.)	Commander
Mr. P. H. Owen	Cadet
Mr. W. Owens	Marine
Mr. G. E. T. Parham	Sergeant, R.M.
Lieutenant R. P. Pirie, R.N. (Retd.)	Midshipman
Engineer Commander J. W. Renshaw, O.B.E., R.N. (Retd.)	Engineer Commander
Mr. S. R. Saltmarsh	Marine

Mr. A. W. Scarff	Petty Officer (Admiral's Coxswain)
Commander C. E. L. Sclater, D.S.O., R.N. (Retd.)	Lieutenant
Lieutenant A. W. Scovell, R.N.	Boy
Stores Chief Petty Officer F. G. Sims, R.N.	Leading Supply Assistant
Mr. G. L. Trewinnard	Boy
Mr. C. J. Wilson	Chief Engine-room Artificer

and, of course, Skipper J. G. Gatt, D.S.C., master of the *Daisy II*. While in hospital, Mr. Kerr wrote down the stories of the following additional survivors: Chief Stoker P. Terry, Marine Moore, Stoker W. M. Campbell, Stoker A. Bond, Stoker O. L. Fletcher, Musician J. F. P. Thompson, Able Seaman W. Hancock, and Ordinary Seaman J. V. Hearn; I have drawn upon these.

For the accounts of what happened in H.M.S. *Pegasus* I am indebted to Mr. E. Bilton, Mr. F. H. Burchett and Mr. R. A. Rowley; and for what happened in H.M.H.S. *Aba,* to Surgeon Commander St. George B. Delisle Gray, V.R.D., R.N.V.R. (Retd.); also to Mr. D. J. Wayland, of the *Voltaire*.

I have also to thank Captain W. R. Fell, R.N. (Retd.) and Mr. J. L. McKay, naval diver, for their recollections of the 1951 Survey; Mr. E. Wheeler, for his account of what happened in the Admiralty water carrier *Fountain* at Lyness; Mr. D. H. Allan, formerly a Police Constable at Kirkwall, for his recollections and much help besides in obtaining from Merchant Navy sources authoritative opinions on Kirk Sound; to Mrs. B. Gunn, of 2, Duncan Street, Thurso, for her memories of that "dark winter's night" when the survivors were brought to her door; and to Mr. E. W. Marwick, Editor of *The Orkney Herald,* for letting me have the results of his researches into the stories of "The Watchmaker of Kirkwall" as well as generously allowing me space in which to contact local witnesses. I have also to thank, for their help in contacting survivors, the Editor of *The Evening News,* Portsmouth, the Editor of *The Sunderland Echo & Shipping Gazette,* and the Editor of *The Evening Express,* Aberdeen.

I am also indebted to the following sources for the German version: the section on Scapa Flow operation in the log of U.47, published in English translation as part of "The Führer Conferences on Naval Affairs" in *Brassey's Naval Annual,* 1948; the section on sinking of the *Norfolk* in the log of U.47, published in English translation, together with some details on the Scapa Flow operation, in *The Gathering Storm,* by Winston Churchill (Cassel); Prien's autobiography, published in English translation as *I Sank the Royal Oak* (Grays Inn Press, 1954); planning of the operation, published in English translation as part of *The Dönitz Memoirs* (Weidenfeld & Nicolson, 1959); some additional details on the planning of the operation, untranslated, appear in *Der Stier von Scapa Flow,* by Wolfgang Frank (Stalling Verlag, 1958).

In conclusion, I must express my gratitude to a number of relatives of those who lost their lives in H.M.S. *Royal Oak,* for help which they were able to give me in various ways; I must mention in particular Mrs. Constance Avery, of Southsea, who lost a brother, Mrs. Audrey Osborne, of Portsmouth, who lost her father, and Mr. T. Jackson, of Houghton-le-Spring, County Durham, who lost his son. I hope that this book will, in some measure, be a memorial to them and their comrades.

The following lists of survivors from the *Royal Oak* are given here exactly as they were issued by the Admiralty on the same day that the ship sank. Inevitably, errors resulted.

FIRST LIST

Lieut. A. M. Seymour
Pay. Cadet M. Holligan
Wt. Engineer G. Dunstone
Petty Officer P. Higgins
Petty Officer E. A. Rowland
Able Seaman C. B. McCabe
Leading Seaman A. Harmer
Ord. Seaman E. Smith
Ord. Seaman Crichton
Ord. Seaman R. Martin
Boy E. W. Scovell
Chief Stoker C. Hine
Stoker H. P. Cleverley
Cook G. R. Stares
Marine J. W. Woods

SECOND LIST

Lieut. G. O. Roberts
Wt. Shipwright W. E. Harding
Comd. Gunner J. T. Pearce

Petty Officer J. R. Kerr
Leading Seaman H. J. Instance
Able Seaman William Hancox
Able Seaman Alfred Elmes
Able Seaman John Ross
Ordinary Seaman V. Marchant
Boy David Belben
Boy Jack Bromyard
Yeo. Sigs. William C. Mitchell
Stoker William Tate
Stoker Oswald L. Fletcher
Ordnance Artificer Hector Randell
Ordnance Artificer Edward Dommett
E.R.A. 5th Class Brocker
E.R.A. 5th Class A. Hastings
E.R.A. 5th Class D. Blackmor
E.R.A. 5th Class E. Jacobs
E.R.A. 5th Class Robert Hayhow
Corporal R.M. Arthur D. Ketcher
Marine Brinley A. Pritchard
Marine James A. Hartley

Marine Edwin J. Fidler
Supply P.O. Norman Finley
S.B.A. Reginald Bendell
P.O. Steward John Ferrugi
Steward Laurence Mallis
Ordinary Seaman James V. Hearn

THIRD LIST

Capt. W. G. Benn
Cdr. R. F. Nicholls
Pay. Cdr. John R. Cundall
Second Lieut. Douglas R. Wheeler
Mid. Ronald M. Seaburn-May
Lieut. Anthony H. Terry
Surgeon-Lieut. Dick Caldwell
Lieut. Henry Duncan
Lieut.-Cdr. Frederick N. Cook
Lieut. Richard S. Wallace
S. Lieut. Anthony H. Pearman
Senior Master George Prowse
Mid. Norman W. Rockingham
Cadet Peter H. Owen
S. Lieut. Frederick Combes
Pay. Lieut. Anthony P. Wilkinson
Gunner Edward A. Evans
Wt. Engineer Frank J. Bulley
Wt. Engineer Edward Whitbread
Bosn. Frank Williams
Lieut. Gerald Affleck-Graves
Pay. Lieut.-Cdr. Qeardley G. S. MacLean
Lieut.-Cdr. Thomas F. Wisden
Surgeon-Cdr. George L. Ritchie
Lieut.-Cdr. Michael R. F. Ward
Lieut.-Cdr. Richard A. V. Gregory
Lieut.-Cdr. James P. Ingpen
S. Lieut. Peter Richard
Lieut. Claude E. L. Sclater
Pay. Lieut. William E. Sandifer
S. Lieut. Kenneth B. Clayton
S. Lieut. Jeffrey T. E. Vincent
Pay. S. Lieut. Gilbert S. Harrison
Mid. John K. Smithalls
Pay. Cadet Michael G. H. Mawson

S. Lieut. (E) Wm. M. Hutchison
Eng. Cdr. J. W. Renshaw
Lieut. Bernard B. Keen
Comd. Gunner Benjamin J. Anslow
Lieut. Michael H. Benton (R.M.)
Pay. Lieut.-Cdr. Arthur F. Blowers
Sig. Bsn. James G. Warren
Act. W.S.O. Gwyn Protheroe
Pay. Lieut. Harold J. C. Woods
Mid. Roger P. Pirie
E.R.A. 5 William A. Dunne
Chief Stoker Philip Terry
S.V. Boy George Trewinnard
Off. C.K.I. Poalo Spitari
Off. C.K.3 Edward Sammit
Ord. Seaman Norman Lazell
Steward Arthur Chalker
Stoker I. John Henry Makin
Able Seaman Samuel Borchwick
Able Seaman John Murray
Marine William Smith
Marine John Breen
Marine Barry Hawes
Marine James W. D. Shuter
Marine Henry J. Goodson
Able Seaman Samuel P. Head
Lead. Cook Frederick J. Ransome
Lead. Cook Frederick S. Clements
Lead. Cook Rufas Baker
Lead. Cook Henry C. Balch
Able Seaman Thomas J. Foster
Lead. Seaman John Harty
Lead. Seaman William A. Edwards
Marine Bertram H. Hilkin
Lead. Seaman Alfred T. Pitcher
Seaman R.N.R. Edward S. Stewart
Ord. Seaman Ronald Kitchener
Able Seaman Tom S. Coulson
Boy L/C. Gordon E. Dove
Ord. Seaman William F. Sidley
Ord. Seaman Alfred Hickmore
C.P.O. Cook Joseph F. Peay
P.O. Albert E. Seymour
Ord. Seaman William A. Lawrence

Boy Ronald V. Harbord
Boy Arthur Smith
Lead. Tel. James R. Melrose
Tel. Frederick L. Hawks
Tel. Robert C. Grove
Boy Tel. Ernest F. Upham
Sig. Kenneth G. Conway
Lead. Tel. Raymond S. Jones
Boy L/C. Frank McCarthy
Lead. Seaman Edward J. Harris
Lead. Seaman William P. Casey
Ord. Seaman Ronald D. Burton
Ord. Seaman Ivor H. Pagett
Able Seaman Peter J. Morris
Ord. Seaman Robert M. Ward
L.S.A. Frank C. Sims
E.R.A. George W. C. Atmeare
Marine Desmond P. O'Byrne
Cadet Seaman George Smith
Cadet Seaman Matthew Bowes
Cadet Seaman Leonard Seal

FOURTH LIST

Ord. Seaman Allen D. Brown
Boy 1st Class Clarence J. Hall
E.R.A. 5 James T. Whitlock
Able Seaman Ellis Clarke
Boy 1st Class Douglas Newton
Boy 1st Class Albert V. Frost
Marine Aubrey S. Amer
Marine Frank White
Marine Alfred J. Wheatland
Marine Thomas R. Drew
Stoker Robert Lees
Stoker James Burnside
Stoker Cecil J. Lucking
Stoker Norman Butcher
Stoker Edward Fleming
E.R.A. James A. Coade
Cpl. R.M. John J. Coombes
Cpl. R.M. John A. Payton
Marine Jack L. Halford
Boy Edward R. Britt
C.E.R.A. Cyril J. Wilson

Ord. Seaman George P. Stephen
Sgt. R.M. George E. T. Parham
Lead. Cook James D. F. O'Leary
Asst. Cook Thomas W. R. Taylor
Lead. Cook Leonard Bryan
Cpl. R.M. George H. Woolnough
Marine Jack E. Bryant
Stoker P.O. Gordon Whitehouse
Stoker P.O. William G. Spurling
Stoker P.O. John Wm. Welch
Blacksmith Arthur R. F. Gibbs
Marine William Hughlock
Lead. Stoker Charles W. T. Murrin
Marine Leslie H. Tunnicliffe
Painter Edgar L. Scott
Ch. Shpt. Reginald W. G. Whincup
Joiner Frederick W. Wiltshire
C.P.O. Wtr. Stanley W. H.
   Thompson
Marine A. Lawrence Archer
C.P.O. George F. Vennel
(?) Walter G. Palmer
Boy L/C. Donald J. Hart
Able Seaman Arthur Brierley
Able Seaman Herbert Wright
Marine Michael F. Davey
Musc. George B. Williams
Boy 1st Class Frank O'N. Dall
Boy 1st Class Ronald C. Green
A.G. Roger Ashley

FIFTH LIST

Marine Kenneth J. J. Wood
Lead. Seaman Henry G. Symonds
Able Seaman Alfred H. Bevis
Lead. Stoker George A. Langlands
Stoker 2nd Class Douglas W. V.
   Sheldrick
Stoker 2nd Class Robert H. Bate-
   man
Lead. Stoker Kenneth Hickman
Stoker Eric E. Lidget
Able Seaman Arthur Gearing
Stoker Reginald Morley

Boy Reuben W. Askham
Lead. Seaman Fred Cross
Ord. Seaman Herbert H. Potts
Marine Ronald Joran
Marine Frederick Hanharan
Lead. Sig. William J. Forsey
Stoker P.O. William A. Cripps
Off. Std. Paulo Zarb
Boy 1st Class George R. White
Marine Thomas W. Potter
Ord. Seaman Stanley Cole
Boy. Tel. Kenneth Harrington
Able Seaman William H. Smart
Boy 1st Class Arthur W. Smith
Able Seaman John Farquhar
Able Seaman Sydney Evans
Able Seaman John E. Hasler
L.S.A. William G. Batterbury
Lead. Wtr. Kenneth H. Willoughby
W.L. Wtr. Leonard Childs
Able Seaman Ernest E. Davis
Able Seaman Henry W. Pither
Marine Frederick A. Martin
Boy Henry P. T. Cox
Boy Albert R. Turney
Boy Gordon F. Cook
Ord. Seaman John T. Lettin
Boy Reginald P. Watten
Boy Arthur Allridge
Cpl. R.M. Norman T. Davies
Able Seaman Edward C. Alford
Cpl. R.M. Herbert Pattison
E.R.A. Ronald Connor
Boy Victor R. Thompson
Ord. Seaman Kenneth E. Davidson
Able Seaman Percy Neville
Able Seaman George A. Smith
Marine Arthur G. Coote
Ch. Stoker Alfred Lawrence
Ch. Stoker Frederick J. Hobbs
Mech. William H. Throssell
Able Seaman James E. Hollis
C.E.R.A. Charles P. Cartwright
Able Seaman George F. Baker

SIXTH LIST

Able Seaman R.F.R. Frank Cutler
Ord. Tel. James Charles Devlyn
P.O. Tel. Thomas H. Lakin
E.R.A. 4 Ronald Hall
Musc. Charles S. Bignell
Marine Albert E. Tutton
Able Seaman Alfred J. Farley
Lead. Seaman David J. Lloyd
Lead. Seaman Reginald C. Green
Lead. Seaman Reginald H. Finlayson
Able Seaman Mac. Williams
Lead. Seaman Allen J. Babb
Lead. Seaman George R. Poling
Able Seaman Henry Pipes
Yeo. Sigs. Ronald S. Howell
R.P.O. John H. Smith
Able Seaman William E. Woodnutt
S.B.C.P.O. Clifford Westcott
Ord. Seaman George L. J. Lockyer
S.B.C.P.O. Henry W. Main
Lead. Stoker John Coady
Boy Ronald E. Wilson
Musc. Alfred L. Fordham
Act. Cpl. R.M. George R. Andrews
Able Seaman Kenneth B. Forder
Marine Arthur J. Moppett
Marine William Owens
Able Seaman R.N.R. James Ross
Seaman R.N.R. Thomas Merrick
Boy William Weir
Able Seaman R.F.R. Wilfred Nichols
Boy John Hall
Boy Herbert E. Pocock
Boy Stanley W. Haigh
Ord. Seaman Charles H. Riley
O.S. 1st Class Anthony Camenzul
Lead. Seaman George J. Maggs
Lead. Seaman Alfred J. Hoskin
P.O. George J. Childs
P.O. (Pens.) Arthur W. Scarff

Stoker 1st Class Reginald A. Pope
A/Lead. Seaman James D. Haig
Lead. Stoker John W. J. Clayton
Lead. Seaman James A. Radford
A/P.O. Victor Cruse
Marine Alexander R. Howard
P.O. Ernest J. Gilmore
Boy John P. Billingham
Ord. Seaman Lawrence W. Milligan
Able Seaman George R. Arnell
Able Seaman Victor L. T. Ayles
P.O. Thomas B. Stevens
Able Seaman Walter Thomas Weare
Stoker 1st Class John Brown
Stoker 1st Class Albert Bond
Musc. R.M. John F. P. Thompson
C.P.O. O.K. William E. Humby
Boy 1st Class Stanley R. Wood
Stoker 1st Class William M. Campbell
Act/P.O. William J. Bardsdell
Marine Edward A. Moore
P.O. Tel. Thomas A. Noble
Lead. Stoker Thomas H. Jones
Marine Norman J. Hine
Ord. Seaman Donald T. Harris
Marine Stanley Rowlands
Boy Kenneth H. Took
Ord. Seaman Dennis W. Masters
Ord. Seaman Eric D. Densham
Ord. Seaman Philip A. White
Boy 1st Class Matthew Skilling
Ord. Seaman Richard H. Gardiner
Boy 1st Class Cyril G. Lipscombe
Ord. Seaman Thomas G. Bishop
Able Seaman Ronald J. Kenny
Joiner Edward Randall
Musc. Cyril S. Poultney
Marine Richard H. Wood
Boy 1st Class John N. Mead
Able Seaman Frederick M. Gattrell
Musc. R.M.B. Horace A. G. Kelly

E.R.A. Edwin H. Fairney
Lead. Stoker George E. Winterbottom
Lead. Stoker Henry J. Lutman

SEVENTH LIST

G. H. E.R.A. Norman V. Pead
Cpl. R.M. James McLaverty
Marine Norman W. Grant
P.O.O.K. James Chalder
R.P.O. Walter G. Phillips
Ch. Stoker William H. Aplin
E.R.A. 4 Robert Edmunds
Sgt. R.M. George H. Booth
Marine Frank Brooke
Able Seaman (Pens.) Henry Bryant
Marine Gerald Ellis
Able Seaman Sidney R. Dawson
Lead. Seaman Jesse Sherwood
Act/P.O. Thomas W. A. Blundell
Lead. Seaman R.N.R. John R. Goodlad
Able Seaman Joseph Figg
Ord. Seaman Norman L. Hinde
Lead. Seaman Harry Farmer
O.C.I. Williams E. Chown
P. C. Std. Alfred G. Ings
Sig. William K. Hutchings
E.R.A. 3 William A. Marsh
Ch. Mech. (Pens.) Jack Timms
Ch. Mech. (Pens.) Robert L. Adams
Ch. Mech. Thomas F. Freer
Marine Richard H. Orges
Marine Norman E. Thackeray
Marine Ronald S. Miles
Marine Alex. G. Chatfield
Able Seaman David H. Ward
Stoker William Cowen
Lead. Seaman Edward A. Boxall
Stoker Harry V. Dowling
Stoker Thomas Harland
Stoker Herbert R. Johnston
Musc. (Deal) Fernleigh G. Judge

C.P.O. Kenneth G. Dewey
Able Seaman Jim Collier
Musc. (Deal) Harold J. Wernham
Musc. Philip C. W. Combes
Stoker P.O. Walter Barrett
Musc. Dennis S. Cook
S.B.P.O. William S. Brigden
Marine Reginald A. Turner
Marine Stanley R. Saltmarsh
Lieut. K. R. S. Leadley, R.N.
Mid. P. D. Sturdee, R.N.
P.O. (Pens.) Reginald G. Sylvester
Stoker 1st Class Ronald Frank Stimson
E.R.A. 5th Class Edward Harris
Able Seaman Alfred Redman, R.N.R.
Lead. Seaman John Atter
Tel. Norman Claude Robertson
O. Sig. Ian Bell
Ord. Seaman Reginald George Birch
Stoker Andrew Paterson
Able Seaman Maurice Blake
Chief E.R.A. Wilfred Gibson

Able Seaman George William Fisher
St. 1 Michael Connelly
Able Seaman Arthur H. Knott
Ord. Tel. Robert E. Jackson

EIGHTH LIST

C.P.O. Mech. H. Bish
P.O. C. W. Ball
Lead. Seaman R. Tily
E.R.A. W. H. Crowther
E.R.A. T. R. Storar
Stoker P. Rose
Stoker H. F. Wadham
Able Seaman R. Anderson
Able Seaman H. J. Woods
Able Seaman H. S. Le-Poidevin
Stoker H. Howe
Tel. W. H. Clark
Able Seaman L. H. Roberts
Sig. J. H. Lee
Sub-Lieut. Kersley, R.N.R.
Mid. W. T. J. Fox
Mid. M. F. J. Symes-Thompson
Stoker P.O. Sydney Henry Cook

Index